Contents

Unit 1 Media institutions **4**
  1.1 Defining the media 4
  1.2 Media organisations 5

Unit 2 Ownership and control of the media **8**
  2.1 Pluralism 8
  2.2 Pluralism – an evaluation 10
  2.3 Marxism 13
  2.4 Ideology and the media 16
  2.5 The new media 16

Unit 3 Selection and presentation of media content **22**
  3.1 The construction of news 22
  3.2 The news and moral panics 25

Unit 4 Media representations **29**
  4.1 Representations and stereotypes 29
  4.2 Representations of gender 30
  4.3 Representations of ethnicity 33
  4.4 Representations of social class 35
  4.5 Representations of age 37
  4.6 Representations of sexuality 38
  4.7 Representations of disability 39

Unit 5 Media effects **41**
  5.1 Two views of media effects 41
  5.2 Case studies of media effects 43

Unit 6 Globalisation **46**
  6.1 What is globalisation? 46
  6.2 Globalisation and the media 47

Unit 7 Postmodernism **49**
  7.1 Postmodern society and the media 49
  7.2 Postmodernism and the media – evaluation 50

References **52**

Author index **53**

Subject index **54**

MASS MEDIA

Introduction

Can you imagine a day going by without watching a television programme or a film on video or DVD; listening to music on the radio, CD or the Internet; or reading a newspaper, magazine or book? If your answer is yes then you're a pretty unusual person! We live in a world where we are surrounded by print and electronic media and depend upon them for information and entertainment.

Use of the media is huge and still growing. In 2001, 55% of adults in the United Kingdom read a daily newspaper and on average spent nearly three hours a day watching television. In addition to these well-established communications media, more and more people have access to new media products. In 2003, 83% of households owned CD players and 45% had access to the Internet. At the same time, the proportion of adults, especially those aged between 15 and 24, attending the cinema at least once a month has grown in the last few years. And the purchase of DVD players and DVDs has increased rapidly (*Social Trends*, 2005).

Television programmes and other media products are produced by organisations. Does it matter who owns and controls these organisations?

We rely upon the media for much of our information and entertainment. Are the media giving us an accurate picture of the world? What images of men and women, for example, are being presented?

We watch, listen to and read media messages. How do audiences respond to these? Do the media have significant effects upon us?

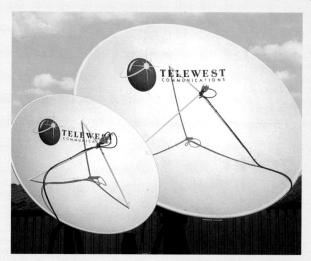

Telewest satellite dishes

Unit 1 Media institutions

keyissues

1 What are the key characteristics of the media?

2 Who owns and controls media institutions?

1.1 Defining the media

What are the mass media? The term *media* describes different means of communication. Some media – such as the telephone – enable communication between two people. However, others allow communication with a *mass* audience. These include newspapers, television, radio, and the Internet.

For much of human history, social relations have been face to face. People communicated by talking and through body language. Now technological developments have made it possible to communicate with large numbers of people at one time. It is these forms of communication that have come to be known as the *mass media*.

'The mass media are simply the means through which content, whether fact or fiction, is produced by organisations and transmitted to and received by an audience' (McCullagh, 2002).

This definition identifies three key aspects of the mass media.

- The production of messages by media institutions

- The content of media messages

- The reception of messages by audiences.

While these three dimensions are interrelated, it is important that each is examined separately. We cannot understand what factors shape media content without looking at the production process. We cannot understand the meanings of media messages without analysing their content. And we cannot reach an informed judgement about media effects without examining how audiences interpret media messages.

We shall examine each of these processes in turn, beginning with media organisations.

1.2 Media organisations

Types of media organisation There are three forms of media organisation.

- Community-based media organisations, eg a radio station in a local hospital
- Public/state owned media organisations, eg the BBC
- Privately owned media organisations, eg News Corporation (Devereux, 2003).

While all three forms still survive, privately-owned media organisations are by far the most significant. Community-based media continue to play a minor role, usually appealing to limited local audiences. Public/state owned media organisations, although in an earlier media age often enjoying a national monopoly, have steadily lost their dominance. They have either been privatised or face significant competition from a limited number of privately-owned global media institutions.

activity1 defining the mass media

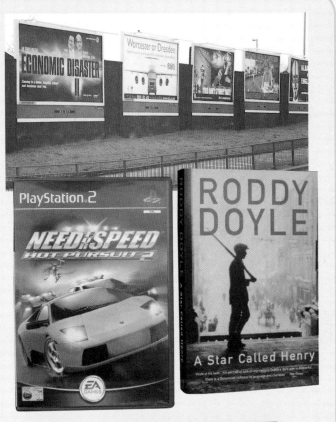

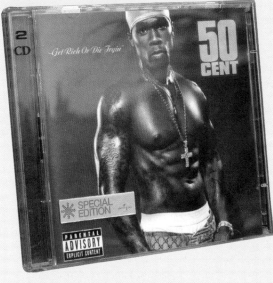

question

Why is each picture an example of the mass media?

Trends in media ownership

Increasing media choice? In the last fifteen years there has been a rapid increase in the range of media outlets. 'In 1988 there were four TV channels in the UK; today over 70; there were sixty commercial radio stations, today 260; 14 cinema multiplexes, today 143; zero web pages, today a billion' (Peake, 2002). These changes suggest a much wider range of choice. However, the source of these 'choices' is a smaller and smaller number of extremely large and powerful media institutions. And, as the next unit indicates, some researchers see this development as reducing choice.

Increasing concentration of media organisations 'Fewer and fewer large companies increasingly own what we see, hear and read' (Williams, 2003). This process is known as the *concentration of media organisations*.

The increasing concentration of media organisations is the result of three major developments:

- Vertical integration
- Horizontal integration and multi-media ownership
- The expansion of transnational organisations.

Let's take each in turn.

Vertical integration This refers to 'the process by which one owner acquires all aspects of production and distribution of a single type of media product' (Croteau & Hoynes, 1997). Vertical integration is not new. Production and distribution of movies were concentrated in the hands of the big five Hollywood companies in the early part of the twentieth century. This enabled them to build a dominant position in world film production. Although film industries subsequently developed elsewhere, Hollywood still retains its dominance. 'The most comprehensive survey of cinema-going in Britain…by the Film Council reveals that although younger people are flocking to the cinema in ever increasing numbers, they are overwhelmingly watching films made by the big US studios' (Kennedy, 2003).

Horizontal integration This refers to 'the process by which one company buys different kinds of media, concentrating ownership across different kinds of media' (Croteau & Hoynes, 1997). Horizontal integration has developed rapidly in recent years. The largest media groups own a range of media. Take News Corporation whose top executive is Rupert Murdoch. Although this company initially produced newspapers, it now has interests in a range of other media, including book and magazine publishing (eg, Harper Collins), television (eg, BSkyB), radio (eg, Sky), film (eg, 20th Century Fox), as well as sports franchises (eg, the Los Angeles Dodgers baseball team).

Transnational ownership The major media organisations operate across national boundaries. Take News Corporation again. Although this company originated in Australia, it now operates on a global scale. It produces over 175 newspapers in Australia, Britain, the USA and Asia; it owns 37 television stations; and it is able to beam programmes into homes through its control of cable programming and satellite operations across Europe, Asia, Australia, Latin America and the USA.

Explaining increasing concentration

Media products such as newspapers and films are costly to produce. They require a large upfront investment. But while producing the first newspaper or film is expensive, the cost of reproducing copies is cheap. This encourages media organisations to maximise their audiences. Hence the three developments outlined above – all of which have led to increasing concentration.

Vertical integration has enabled Hollywood companies to sell their films more easily. Horizontal integration has allowed organisations to promote their products across a range of media. 'Batman was developed into a film publicised by Time Warner through its magazines and promoted via its cable and television networks, the soundtrack of which was released on its record labels and whose merchandising included children's toys produced through its manufacturing interests' (Williams, 2003).

What is more, the development of multi-media organisations operating across the world enables them to search for markets on a global scale. 'The marketing of *The Lion King, Pocahontas*, and many other animated characters, by Walt Disney (the film, the dolls, the books, the jigsaw puzzles, lunchboxes and so on) is but one of many examples of this (worldwide) exploitation of one product in as many markets as possible' (Newbold et al., 2002).

key terms

Mass media Means of communication through which content – news, sport, music, drama, writing, advertising – are transmitted to large audiences.

Media concentration The concentration of mass media ownership into fewer and fewer organisations.

Vertical integration One company acquiring all aspects of the production and distribution of a single type of media product.

Horizontal integration One organisation buying up companies from different media, concentrating ownership across different kinds of media.

Transnational ownership The ownership by a single company of media organisations which operate in two or more countries.

summary

1. The mass media are the means of communication through which messages are produced by organisations and received by audiences.

2. Most people use the mass media extensively for information and entertainment.

3. Ownership and control of the mass media has become increasingly concentrated in recent years due to vertical integration, horizontal integration and transnational ownership.

activity2 media concentration

Item A National newspaper ownership in the UK

Group name	Market share (%)	Title control	Executive
News International (part of News Corporation)	37.2	*Sun* *Times* *Sunday Times* *News of the World*	Rupert Murdoch
Trinity Mirror	20.5	*Daily Mirror* *Sunday Mirror* *People*	Victor Blank
Daily Mail and General Trust	18.7	*Daily Mail* *Mail on Sunday*	Lord Rothermere
Northern and Shell	9.6	*Daily Express* *Daily Star* *Sunday Express*	Richard Desmond
Hollinger International	7.0	*Daily Telegraph* *Sunday Telegraph*	Conrad Black
Guardian Media Group	3.3	*Guardian* *Observer*	The Scott Trust
Pearson	1.9	*Financial Times*	Pearson Board
Independent News and Media	1.8	*Independent* *Independent on Sunday*	Tony O'Reilly

Adapted from Peake, 2002

Item B Media concentration in the USA

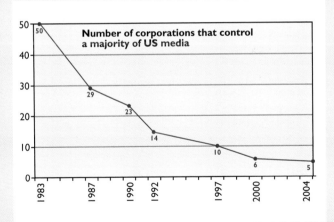

The 5 corporations which controlled most of the mass media in the USA in 2004 were AOL Time Warner, Disney, Viacom, News Corporation and Bertelsmann.

Adapted from Bagdikian, 2004

Item C Media merger

Viacom chairman Sumner Redstone announces the merger between CBS and Viacom in 1999. Viacom, the owner of MTV and Paramount Studios, bought CBS for $36 billion – the most expensive media merger in history.

question

How does each of the items indicate media concentration?

Unit 2 Ownership and control of the media

keyissues

1 Does it matter who owns and controls the media?

2 Do the media provide the information required for an informed citizenship?

What is the relationship between ownership and control of the mass media? To what extent do the owners of media corporations control the content of the media they produce? Does media concentration matter? Are we well served by the mass media on offer? These are some of the questions addressed in this unit. These questions are examined in terms of two sociological theories – pluralism and Marxism.

2.1 Pluralism

Pluralism – the theory

Pluralism is a sociological theory which presents the following picture of Western societies. These societies are seen as *representative democracies* – societies in which the concerns and interests of the population as a whole and of particular groups within the population are represented. The electorate – those entitled to vote – elect politicians whose job is to represent the nation as a whole. The electorate has the freedom to choose between competing political parties.

Pressure groups or interest groups represent sections of the population. For example, there are a range of interest groups representing various occupations – for instance, professional associations such as the British Medical Association representing doctors and trade unions such as the National Union of Teachers representing teachers. Pressure groups, as their name suggests, put pressure on the government to further the interests of their members. Some pressure groups represent more vulnerable groups in society – for example, the Child Poverty Action Group represents the interests of the poor. And, at the other end of the scale, the Confederation of British Industry represents the interests of the owners, managers and shareholders of private industry.

From a pluralist point of view, no one group is dominant in society – to some extent all groups have a say in the running of society, and all adults have the freedom to choose who governs society.

Pluralism and the media

Reflecting public demand The pluralist picture of a representative democracy is reflected in pluralist views of the media. It states that the content of the mass media mirrors what the public, or a section of the public, wants.

The media cater to the public as a whole or to particular groups in society. Put another way, the media simply respond to the demands of the market.

Those who own and control the media usually take a pluralist view, arguing that they must satisfy public demand to stay in business. If they failed to do this, nobody would buy their newspapers or watch their TV programmes.

Diverse society, diverse media The media present a range of views which reflect the diversity of opinions in society. The pluralist theory of power states that no one group dominates the whole of society – power is shared among a range of groups. The mass media mirror this diversity. They present a wide range of views, which allows the audience freedom to choose between them. Minority views and tastes are catered for because of the choice of newspapers, magazines, films, radio and TV channels available in a free market.

The media may be biased in certain ways but this is simply because the views they broadcast are those that most people sympathise with and want to hear. If asylum seekers are represented as a 'problem', it is because this reflects the majority view; if women are portrayed in domestic roles, this reflects the reality of most women's lives.

Media concentration Does media concentration matter? Are we, the audience, well served by the concentration of ownership and control in the hands of a few, extremely powerful, media magnates?

Many pluralists argue that concentration of ownership is essential for survival in an increasingly global market. Only global companies such as AOL Time Warner, Viacom and News International have the resources to provide audiences with a wider choice and a greater range of media products at affordable prices. Increasing media concentration should therefore be welcomed (Curran & Seaton, 1997).

Media deregulation In many countries there are laws which regulate the ownership and content of the media. For example, in the UK, television broadcasts were formerly limited to the BBC, a state-owned organisation controlled by a board of governors appointed by the Home Secretary. The content of broadcasts was regulated by the rules of public service broadcasting which stated that the BBC should 'inform, educate and entertain'. In practice, this meant a balance between entertainment on the one hand and news and documentaries on the other hand.

From 1954, with the introduction of commercial television, there has been steady reduction of the regulations governing the media. This process is known as *media deregulation*. In terms of television, this has resulted in a rapid expansion in the number of channels and increased competition between terrestrial, satellite and cable companies. The rules governing programme content have been reduced – for example, MTV is clearly not bound by the requirements of public service broadcasting.

In most countries, there are laws which limit the concentration of media ownership. They are designed to prevent organisations from dominating large sections of the media. In recent years, these laws have been relaxed. This is a further example of media deregulation.

In general, pluralists welcome media deregulation. They argue that private ownership of the media is the most effective way to provide a wide range of choice. Privately-owned media organisations compete with each other to give audiences what they want. If audiences reject their products, they would go out of business. By contrast, publicly-owned media and state regulation can be seen as dangerous since they concentrate too much power in the hands of government, offer limited choice and are unresponsive to their audience.

key terms

Pluralism A theory which sees power widely dispersed in democratic societies.

Representative democracy A system of government in which the people are represented by elected officials.

Media deregulation The reduction or abolition of laws limiting media ownership and regulating media output.

activity3 catering for all tastes

Item A Girls' and lads' magazines

Item B Minority ethnic media

Red Records, Brixton, South London, specialising in African-Caribbean music

Indian film poster, Brick Lane, East London

Reading The Voice, an African-Caribbean newspaper

question

What support do these items provide for the pluralist view that the media cater for a range of groups in society?

Radio presenter at Sunrise Radio, an Asian radio station

2.2 Pluralism – an evaluation

The previous section outlined pluralist views of the relationship between ownership and control of the media and presented evidence to support those views. This section looks at criticisms of pluralist views.

Media concentration and democracy

In *The New Media Monopoly*, Ben Bagdikian (2004) makes the following criticisms of pluralist views. His evidence is drawn mainly from America.

In 1983, most of the mass media in the USA was owned and controlled by 50 corporations. By 2004, the media was dominated by five giant corporations – AOL Time Warner, Disney, News Corporation, Bertelsmann and Viacom. According to Bagdikian, this increasing media concentration has very serious consequences. It has moved politics in the USA towards the far right – the views broadcast are increasingly conservative and there is little room for liberal or radical voices. These views reflect those of the media owners – and the advertisers on whom the owners depend for their profits.

Media concentration has also resulted in less and less local news and local voices. For example, the largest radio chain has over 1,200 local radio stations but only 200 employees. The programmes are pre-recorded and the same programmes are broadcast by local stations throughout the USA.

Bagdikian argues that both local and national democracy are under threat. Despite more and more TV channels and radio stations, choice has been narrowed since they're all broadcasting more and more of the same thing – more 'reality' shows, more sitcoms and soaps, more movies. There is little diversity of opinion in the news and little access to local TV and radio.

In a democracy, citizens need to be informed – they need a range of views, a variety of opinions and information from which to make informed choices. Broadcast media are required by law to operate 'in the public interest'. According to Bagdikian, they are failing to do this and, in the process, failing to produce the informed voters essential for a democracy.

The drive for profits

In the UK, the BBC is funded by a licence fee. All other broadcasting media – commercial TV and radio – are funded by advertising (eg, ITV) or subscription (eg, BSkyB). As a public service broadcaster, the BBC is required to 'inform, educate and entertain'. The information it broadcasts should be 'accurate and impartial' and it should produce a variety of programmes to cater for all groups in society. OFCOM – the Office for Communications – regulates the output of both the BBC and commercial broadcasters. As with ownership, the rules governing the content of broadcasting have been relaxed. For example, TV channels can now specialise in popular music (eg, MTV), sport (eg, Sky Sports 1 and 2) or shopping (eg, the Shopping Channel).

Privately-owned commercial broadcasters are in business to make money. Their primary aim is profit rather than public service. And this is the main influence on media content. Evidence to support this view is given in the following examples.

Infotainment The need to make more money by increasing readership of newspapers has led to the growth of the 'human interest' story. This has largely replaced political coverage in the tabloid press (McCullagh, 2002). Now news has become 'infotainment' – part of the entertainment industry. Gossip about the 'instant stars' created by reality TV programmes such as *Big Brother* is regularly reported in tabloid newspapers. Investigative journalists have been replaced by celebrity columnists and presenters (Franklin, 1997).

Advertising revenue The importance of advertising as a major source of revenue has encouraged media organisations to focus on audiences with significant purchasing power. This means mass audiences – in general, the larger the audience the higher the advertising fees – or smaller audiences with spending power such as the young people who watch MTV and the readership of 'quality' newspapers such as the *Times* and *Telegraph*. This has led to a decline in the number of newspapers and minority interest programmes whose audiences are relatively poor (Curran & Seaton, 1997).

At the same time, the boundary between media content and advertising is being broken down (Murdock, 1992). For example, companies pay for products to be 'placed' in films. And companies who sponsor TV programmes sometimes become part of the show – for example, Nokia's sponsorship of the *X-Factor* with its adverts, 'love your music, love your Nokia'.

The influence of proprietors

The pluralist view argues that the power of media proprietors (owners) to influence media content is limited by their need to make profits. If proprietors printed or broadcast views which did not reflect those of their audience, then they may well go out of business.

How much do proprietors influence the content of the media they produce? Answers to this question fall into two main approaches – the *instrumental* and the *structural* approach.

The instrumental approach This approach argues that the proprietors of media organisations directly influence the content of the media they own. Between the two world wars, press barons such as Lord Rothermere and Lord Beaverbrook used their newspapers to put across conservative political views. Some researchers argue that the growing concentration of the media has increased the power of proprietors who frequently mount propaganda campaigns 'to defend the economic, social and political agenda of privileged groups' (Herman & Chomsky, 1988).

The structural approach This approach also recognises that top media executives exercise considerable power.

However, those who favour this approach argue that it is impossible for one individual to control the day-to-day output of huge media organisations such as Rupert Murdoch's News Corporation. They see Murdoch's power as *allocative control* – the power to set the goals of the organisation and to make key financial decisions (Williams, 2003). In Murdoch's case, key decisions relating to the press have involved:

● Relocating the production of his British newspapers in 1986 from Fleet Street to Wapping, where new technology could be employed to destroy the power of the print unions

● Sacking editors who did not share his views

● Reducing the price of his newspapers to drive out competitors (Eldridge et al., 1997).

Despite the limitations of allocative control, it is still possible for proprietors to express their own views in the media they own. Evidence to support this claim is given in Activity 4.

activity4 the influence of proprietors

Item A Rupert Murdoch

Rupert Murdoch is the owner and chief executive of News Corporation, a global media company worth around $60 billion. Murdoch owns or part-owns terrestrial, cable and satellite television companies which broadcast to North and South America, Europe, Asia and Australasia, film companies, radio stations and a global book publisher – HarperCollins.

Murdoch also owns 175 newspapers on three continents. They publish 40 million papers a week and dominate the newspaper markets in Britain, Australia and New Zealand. In an interview in his own *Sydney Daily Telegraph*, Murdoch backed President Bush's stance against Saddam Hussein and called for war against Iraq. And the editors of his 175 newspapers around the world mirrored his views, supporting military action against Saddam.

Adapted from *The Guardian*, 17.2.2003 and *The Independent*, 18.10.2004

Item B Conducting his campaign

This graphic by Steve Caplin gives one view of Murdoch's campaign for war against Iraq.

Item C What his papers say

The tyranny of Saddam and the danger to innocent lives demand the world responds.

Sydney Daily Telegraph

There comes a time when evil must be stopped, and it is better to do that sooner rather than later.

Brisbane Courier-Mail

The doubters must say how much more time they would give Saddam to play his delaying games.

Wellington Dominion-Post

Stick with the friend you can trust through and through – America.

The Sun

Item D Murdoch's leadership style

Richard Searby, one-time chairman of News Corporation, describes Rupert Murdoch's leadership style.

Most company boards meet to take decisions. Ours meets to ratify – confirm and rubber stamp – Rupert's. For much of the time, you don't hear from Rupert. Then, all of a sudden, he descends like a thunderbolt from hell to slash and burn all before him. Since nobody is ever sure when the next autocratic intervention will take place (or on what subject), they live in fear of it and try to second guess what he would want, even in the most unimportant of matters.

Quoted in *Neill*, 1996

Item E Media concentration and deregulation

The Italian senate has been debating a controversial bill that critics say would enable the prime minister, Silvio Berlusconi, to extend his already formidable influence over the country's media.

The bill would allow Mr Berlusconi's Mediaset television group to keep all three of its channels, enable it to increase substantially its advertising revenue and to buy into the newspaper market.

Directly through Mediaset, in which Mr Berlusconi has a 48.6% stake, and indirectly by way of the state broadcaster, Rai, Italy's prime minister is in a position to influence more than 90% of the country's television output.

The dangers posed by his grip on the media were highlighted last week when the main Rai evening news bulletin failed to broadcast remarks by him that caused uproar across Europe.

These remarks were made during an appearance before the European parliament when Mr Berlusconi told a German MEP (Member of the European parliament), he would be ideal for the part of a concentration camp guard in a film being produced in Italy.

Adapted from *The Guardian*, 9.7.2003

Silvio Berlusconi, centre

question

1 How do Items A, B, C and D support the claim that proprietors directly influence the content of the news media?

2 What support does Item E provide for the argument that media concentration and deregulation are threats to democracy?

activity5 the drive for profits

AND TONIGHT, AS IRAN DECLARES WAR ON CHINA AND UNEMPLOYMENT REACHES SEVEN MILLION, WE ASK, WHAT ABOUT THAT ROYAL DIVORCE?

NEWS 24-7

Adapted from Glasgow Media Group, 1982

question

How does this cartoon suggest that the drive for profits influences media content?

2.3 Marxism

The theory

Karl Marx (1818-1883) argued that human society was made up of two parts – the *infrastructure* or economic base and the *superstructure* which, in capitalist industrial society, includes the political, legal and educational systems, the mass media and beliefs and values. The superstructure is largely shaped by the infrastructure – in other words, the economic base largely shapes the rest of society.

Social classes According to Marx, every society has two main social groups, a *ruling class* and a *subject class*. The power of the ruling class comes from its ownership of what Marx called the *means of production*. This includes the land, raw materials, machinery, tools and buildings used to produce goods. Thus in Western industrial society, *capitalists* – those who own private industry – form the ruling class. The subject class – the *proletariat* – is made up of workers who sell their labour in return for wages.

There is a basic conflict of interest between capitalists and workers. The workers produce wealth in the form of goods yet a large part of that wealth is taken in the form of profits by the capitalist class. Thus one group gains at the expense of the other.

Marx believed that this conflict could not be resolved within the framework of capitalist society. It would eventually result in the overthrow of the capitalist class. A workers' revolution would lead to a communist society in which the means of production would be owned by everyone, classes would disappear, and exploitation and oppression would end.

Ruling class ideology This, however, would only happen when workers became fully aware of their exploitation. But this awareness will not occur overnight because of the way society is structured. Since the infrastructure largely shapes the superstructure, the relationship of dominance and subordination between the ruling class and subject class will be reflected in the superstructure. Thus, the political and legal systems will support ruling class power – for example, laws will protect the rights of capitalists to own industry and take profits. In the same way, the beliefs and values of society will support ruling class domination. Thus, capitalism will be seen as reasonable and just, rather than exploitative and oppressive. In this way, beliefs and values will disguise and distort the true nature of society.

In Marxist terms, beliefs and values form a *ruling class ideology*. This produces a *false consciousness* which prevents people from seeing the reality of their situation.

Marxism and the media

In Marx's words, ' the ruling ideas are the ideas of the ruling class'. As part of the superstructure, the mass media will reflect the economic base and present capitalism as normal, reasonable and acceptable. And, as part of the ruling class, those who own and control the media will have a vested interest in portraying capitalist society in a positive light. As a result, the media transmit a conservative, conformist view, promote established attitudes and values, and reinforce the position of the powerful.

Ideology Ralph Miliband's study *The State in Capitalist Society* (1973) provides an example of a Marxist approach to the media. The ruling class have to convince the rest of the population to accept the widespread inequalities which are inevitable in capitalist societies. Miliband points to the power of the dominant classes to control the way people think through *ideology* – a false view of reality. This control is exercised in part through the mass media.

Miliband rejects the idea of pluralist diversity. He sees the choice of alternative options and ideas presented by the media as very limited. The content of the media reflects the viewpoint of the dominant group in society – the White, male, ruling class. It is not just political reporting that supports the system, the content of entertainment programmes is also seen as supporting the way things are by portraying the capitalist system in a favourable light.

The new 'opium of the people' Miliband describes the media as the new 'opium of the people', adapting Marx's famous phrase, 'religion is the opium of the people'. He sees the media acting like opium, a hallucinatory drug which creates illusions and produces a feeling of well-being. This keeps the working class quiet and encourages them to accept a system which, in reality, exploits them.

In a similar vein, Herbert Marcuse (1964) suggests that programmes which simply entertain, plus the promise of consumer satisfaction that advertisements and game shows provide, help to remove any doubts people may have about the organisation of society. Programmes such as *EastEnders* and *Coronation Street* divert attention from the unfair nature of society, give the impression that nothing is radically wrong with the world we live in, and provide enjoyment and a sense of well-being for millions.

Neo-Marxism and cultural hegemony

The picture presented so far is of a society brainwashed by a pervasive ruling class ideology. There appears to be little or no challenge to this ideology. In particular, the media fail to provide alternative views and critical voices.

Neo-Marxists ('new' Marxists) present a somewhat different picture. They draw on the work of the Italian Marxist, Antonio Gramsci (1891-1937). Gramsci argues that beliefs and ideas are not simply shaped by the economic base. To some extent they have a life of their own.

Cultural hegemony Gramsci refers to the power of ruling class ideology as *cultural hegemony* – the dominance of one set of ideas and beliefs over others. He argues that there are always ideas and beliefs which challenge the dominant ideology and which threaten cultural hegemony. For example, as a result of their experience in capitalist society, workers will, at least partially, see through the

activity6 entertainment

Item A *EastEnders*

Item B *The National Lottery*

question

How might a Marxist interpret Items A and B?

---

dominant ideology and may develop views in opposition to it.

The British sociologist Stuart Hall (1995), has developed Gramsci's argument. He claims that the economic base places real limits on the development of alternative views but it cannot always prevent them. As a result, cultural hegemony is never complete, never totally dominant. To some extent, there are always competing viewpoints, there are always people who challenge dominant beliefs. And these challenges to cultural hegemony can change society.

The media and cultural hegemony To what extent does the media challenge cultural hegemony? Very little, according to researchers such as Ben Bagdikian – see page 10. However, as Activity 7 shows, it is possible to find examples which challenge dominant beliefs.

Marxism – an evaluation

From a Marxist viewpoint, it doesn't particularly matter who owns and controls the mass media – whether it is state owned like the BBC or privately owned like commercial TV. Because of the structure of capitalist society, the media will reflect the views of the capitalist class and broadcast the dominant ideology. Critics have argued that this is not always the case. To some extent, their criticisms have been taken on board by Neo-Marxists who accept that there are challenges to cultural hegemony.

Marxists make a judgement about what they see as the

dominant ideology. They judge it to be a distorted view of reality which serves to disguise the oppression and exploitation of the capitalist system. As purveyors of the dominant ideology, the mass media are seen as instruments of oppression. Clearly, pluralists would reject this view and see it simply as a value judgement, with little or no basis in reality. From a pluralist viewpoint, the media reflect the concerns and interests of all the major groups in society.

key terms

Infrastructure The economic base of society.

Superstructure The rest of society, including the mass media.

Means of production The things used to produce goods – for example, machinery and raw materials.

Ruling class Those who own the means of production.

Subject class Those who actually produce the goods.

Ruling class ideology A false and distorted picture of society which supports the position of the ruling class.

False class consciousness A false picture of the class system which prevents people from seeing the reality of their situation.

Cultural hegemony The dominant ideas and beliefs in society. There are always alternative ideas and beliefs which threaten cultural hegemony.

activity 7 challenging cultural hegemony

Item A Michael Moore

Produced, directed and written by Michael Moore, (holding Bush's hand on the DVD cover), *Fahrenheit 9/11* was a box-office success in cinemas across the USA. It was a scathing attack on the Bush administration. In a nutshell, Bush and those surrounding him were portrayed as liars, cheats and frauds, representing the interests of big business rather than those of the people.

A flavour of the film can be seen from the following example. In 2001, the Bush administration said that Iraq did not present a threat to America or the rest of the world. By 2003, all this changed. Iraq had weapons of mass destruction which threatened world peace and there was a close link between Iraq and al-Qaeda. We now know that neither of these claims was true. Despite this, President Bush stated that the invasion of Iraq in 2003 was 'to save the world from great danger' and to bring democracy and freedom to the Iraqi people. However, *Fahrenheit 9/11* suggests another reason. In the words of one of the participants, 'If it wasn't for the oil, nobody would be there'.

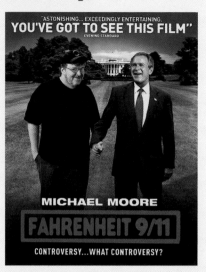

"ASTONISHING... EXCEEDINGLY ENTERTAINING. **YOU'VE GOT TO SEE THIS FILM**"
EVENING STANDARD

MICHAEL MOORE

FAHRENHEIT 9/11

CONTROVERSY...WHAT CONTROVERSY?

Item B Reporting Hurricane Katrina

Thousands of desperate people outside the Superdome in New Orleans waiting to be rescued.

On August 29, 2005, Hurricane Katrina smashed into the Gulf Coast of the USA. Over 1,000 people were killed and over a million made homeless. New Orleans was flooded when the hurricane broke through its sea defences. Over 60 fires blazed in the city and hundreds of people were trapped in bedrooms and on rooftops. The scenes were horrific. One woman tells how she couldn't get the images of dead babies, women and men floating along the streets out of her head.

Ray Nagin, the mayor of New Orleans, described the rescue operation as a 'national disgrace'. Over 50,000 people were trapped in the city for nearly a week with no electricity, sanitation or medical care and very little food and water. People shouted to the TV cameras: 'We're dying.' 'We haven't eaten for days.' 'Doesn't anybody care?' Many of those who got out were stranded for days on a motorway just outside New Orleans. Buses sent to rescue them did not arrive because there were no plans for housing them. The United States government was totally unprepared for a disaster on this scale, despite being warned for years that it was going to happen.

The American media, not known for their critical stance, became increasingly angry and hostile towards the government. The *New York Times* asked 'Who are we if we can't take care of our own?' The same newspaper stated, 'Thousands of Americans are dead or dying, not because they refused to evacuate New Orleans, but because they were too poor or too sick to get out without help – and help wasn't provided.' Jack Cafferty, a veteran newscaster on CNN TV News angrily stated, 'I have never seen anything as bungled and as poorly managed. Where the hell is the water for these people? Why can't sandwiches be dropped? This is a disgrace.'

Media coverage shocked America. Those who suffered most were poor and Black. Nearly a third of the population of New Orleans lived below the poverty line and around 85% of them were Black. The comments of Jesse Jackson, a civil rights leader, were broadcast across America: 'Today, I saw 5,000 African Americans on Highway 10, desperate, perishing, dehydrated, babies crying – it looked like the hold of a slave ship.'

The results of years of racial discrimination and government indifference to the poor were clear for all to see. Questions were increasingly asked about the Bush administration's policy of cutting taxes for the rich and cutting welfare for the poor. George W. Bush, forced to cut short one of his many holidays to make a personal appearance in New Orleans, denied that race was an issue. Even he, faced with TV pictures which said the opposite, was forced to admit that 'poverty has roots in a history of racial discrimination which cut off generations from the opportunity of America.' What was out of sight, out of mind, ignored and brushed under the carpet, now stared mainstream America in the face.

Adapted from various issues of the *Observer* and *Guardian*, September, 2005

question

How can Items A and B be seen as challenges to cultural hegemony in the USA?

2.4 Ideology and the media

The term ideology has been used in many different ways. This section looks at some of those ways.

Marxist views

Marxist views of ideology have been examined in the previous section. They will be summarised briefly here.

A distortion of reality Marxists use the term ideology in a negative sense to describe a set of ideas which distort reality and give a false picture of society.

A justification for inequality Ideology not only distorts reality, it also provides a justification for inequality. For example, it justifies and legitimates the position of the capitalist class and supports its dominance. And it blinds the working class to the truth about their situation. For example, the emphasis on freedom in capitalist society – the free market, free democratic societies, individual freedoms – projects an illusion which disguises the oppression and exploitation of the working class.

Ideology and the media As outlined in the previous section, Marxists see the media as the main transmitter of ideology in capitalist society.

Feminist views

Some, but by no means all, feminists use the term ideology in much the same way as Marxists – it distorts reality and justifies inequality. However, feminists are concerned with gender rather than class inequality. So when they talk about *patriarchal ideology*, they refer to a false picture of the nature of women and men. And this picture serves to justify and maintain gender inequality.

Like Marxists, feminists see ideology as a reflection of power in society. In this case, the powerful are men and, as a result, patriarchal ideology reflects male dominance. Again, like Marxists, they see the media as one of the main ways in which patriarchal ideology is broadcast.

Neutral views of ideology

The views of ideology outlined above are all negative. Ideology is bad, false and oppressive. Neutral views see ideology as neither good nor bad, true nor false, liberating nor oppressive. Many sociologists use the term ideology in a neutral way. Here are some examples.

- Ideology is a set of ideas which guide and direct political action (Heywood, 2002).

- Ideology is a set of values and beliefs shared by a group of people. It explains how society works and how it ought to work (Dobson, 1992).

Liberal ideology

Many sociologists see liberalism, in the broadest sense of the term, as the ideology of modern Western democracies. Pluralists take this point of view. The following are some of the key ideas of liberalism.

Individual freedom The aim of liberalism is to create a society in which every individual is free to develop their own unique talents. Individual freedom is central to liberal thinking. Each person should be able to act as they please, so long as they don't threaten the freedom of others to do likewise.

Equality of opportunity Each individual should have an equal opportunity to develop their talents to the full. This does not mean that everybody should be equal in terms of wealth, income and social status, only that they should have an equal chance to attain positions of power and status.

Liberals believe in equal rights – for example, equality under the law and political equality in the sense of one person, one vote.

Government by consent Government should be based on the consent of the governed – a representative democracy translates this ideal into practice. One of the main tasks of government is to protect individual freedom. Many liberals believe in a form of limited government that protects but does not infringe on the rights and liberties of the individual.

Pluralism, liberalism and the media From a pluralist viewpoint, both the content of the media and the range and variety of media institutions reflect liberal ideology. For example, the liberal views of equality of opportunity and equal rights under the law are reflected in the content of TV programmes and newspaper reports. And the variety of TV channels, newspapers and magazines provides the freedom of choice essential for a democratic society.

Political ideologies These usually refer to the ideologies of political parties. In Western democracies, they are often seen as variations of an overarching liberal ideology.

From a pluralist view, the main political ideologies – Labour, Conservative and Liberal Democrat – are reflected by TV news, which is supposed to be politically neutral. By comparison, daily newspapers tend to support particular political parties. For example, the *Daily Mail* supports the Conservative Party and the *Mirror* supports the Labour Party. Pluralists see the media reflecting and giving voice to the main political ideologies.

2.5 The new media

This section looks at recent developments in the media such as the Internet and satellite broadcasting. It examines some of the key questions addressed in this unit in terms of the new media. For example, is the Internet an instrument for revitalising and expanding democracy – is *e-democracy* a hope for the future? Or does the Internet simply extend the dominance and further the interests of the powerful – will *e-commerce* become a major force in capitalist domination?

Many sociologists believe that we are in the middle of a communications revolution which is transforming the way images, text and sounds are communicated. Three technological developments are seen as particularly important in bringing about this revolution.

- The development of relatively cheap personal computers allowing access to the Internet for millions of people at home and at work
- The emergence of new ways of sending audio-visual signals to individual households
- The growth of digital technology causing changes in the way information (images, texts and sounds) is stored and transmitted.

New media

The Internet, along with cable television and satellite broadcasting, are examples of *new media*. The new media share three characteristics:

- 'They are screen based', with information being displayed on a television screen, PC monitor or a mobile telephone.
- 'They can offer images, text and sounds.'
- 'They allow some form of interaction.' (Collins & Murroni, 1996)

The Internet The Internet is a global system of interconnected computers. It is not owned by any individual or company, but comprises a network that stretches across the world. The best known part of the Internet is the World Wide Web (WWW), effectively a global multi-media library.

The Internet was created in 1969 by the American military to enable scientists working on military contracts across the US to share resources and information. It developed further in the 1980s within universities, but it was not until the second half of that decade, with the increased availability of PCs in the home, that the Internet really took off (Gorman & McLean, 2003). The proportion of households in the UK who owned computers increased from 18 to 34 per cent between 1988 and 1998 and the proportion who have access to the Internet has jumped from under 10 per cent in 1998 to 47 per cent in 2003 (ONS, 2003).

Cable television and satellite broadcasting Terrestrial broadcasting by the BBC and ITV operates by sending audio-visual signals through the air which are picked up by ordinary television aerials. By contrast, cable television relies on a physical cable link and satellite broadcasting on dishes to pick up signals.

In contrast to the US and the rest of Europe, cable television in the UK is less popular than satellite broadcasting. In 2002, only 14.7 per cent of homes in the UK where cable is available had taken out a television subscription. By contrast, a quarter of UK homes have satellite dishes, with the number of subscribers to BSkyB topping 6 million in July 2002 (Peake, 2002). The development of cable television and satellite broadcasting enables people to choose from a much larger number of television channels.

Digitalisation Of central importance to recent technological developments in the media is *digitalisation* – the shift from analogue to digital coding of information. Digital systems translate all information – images, texts, sounds – into a universal computer language. The use of this common language reduces the boundaries between different media sectors. 'Digital transmission technology has a broadcasting capacity many times bigger than analogue, opening the door on a new era: many more TV channels and radio stations; higher quality pictures and sound; multimedia facilities; and interactivity (home shopping, games, video on demand)' (Peake, 2002).

The impact of the new media

Diversity and choice In one respect, the new media have led to more consumer choice. For example, cable television and satellite broadcasting have increased the number of television channels. While many of these are entertainment channels, the number of news channels has also increased. Sometimes these provide views of world affairs that are very different from British and American sources. During the war in Iraq in 2003, the Arab news channel al-Jazeera provided an alternative source of news for viewers in the Arab world.

Quality The government exercises some control over the quality and range of programmes on the BBC and ITV. However, the main providers of cable and satellite broadcasting – NTL, Telewest and BSkyB – face 'no regulatory directives on either the range or the sources of programme material' (Negrine, 1994). Anxious to make as much profit as possible on their massive investments, cable and satellite broadcasters fill their channels with cheap imported material, films, or sport.

Other broadcasting organisations are tempted to follow suit as they too search for large audiences to generate advertising revenue or, in the case of the BBC, to justify the license fee. According to many commentators, 'there is a consequent loss in both the quality, and the range, of programmes produced' (Negrine, 1994). Increased choice does not therefore mean increased diversity.

Inequality There is also inequality of access to the new media. As subscription channels and pay-per-view become more popular, poorer people become excluded from key world events, especially in entertainment and sport.

The public sphere

The media as a public sphere The idea of a *public sphere* refers to a space where people can freely debate issues that are of importance to them as citizens. Habermas (1992) argues that the public sphere emerged in eighteenth century coffee houses where individuals could meet to discuss the issues of the day. This sphere was independent of both commerce and the government. The mass media in Habermas's view threaten this space because they are primarily concerned to make profits. This means they seek to manipulate our thoughts and behaviour in order to make money.

This picture of the mass media has been criticised because

it ignores the pressures on the news media to be 'objective' and does not take account of public service broadcasting. In Britain, for example, the BBC was established as a public service organisation funded by the license fee and obliged to present news and current affairs in an impartial way. While increased competition for readers and viewers has, in the view of many sociologists, led to more 'infotainment', public service broadcasting survives.

The Internet as a public sphere The spectacular growth of the Internet has suggested to some people that the public sphere is being given a new lease of life. There are two main reasons for this.

- In contrast to conventional news media, where editors and journalists define what counts as news, the Internet provides individuals with the opportunity to access a wider range of information and interpretations. Any point of view, no matter how extreme, can be found on the Internet.

- The Internet provides individuals with the opportunity to engage in online discussions and debates across the globe. In contrast to conventional news media, where communication is predominantly one way, the Internet provides a means through which people can interact with others.

The Internet and e-democracy Can the Internet really revitalise democracy? Can people directly participate in the democratic process via the Internet? And can their participation in cyberspace actually change things 'on the ground'?

It's early days yet, but some believe that the answer to these questions is 'eventually, yes'. They argue that the Internet gives voice to those who might otherwise go unheard, it allows like-minded people to join together and take action which may lead to social change, it allows the powers that be to be challenged, it provides a means for citizens to direct communication, send and receive messages, discuss and debate. In other words, it may develop into the public sphere which Habermas believes is lost (Livingstone, 2004). Activity 8 provides examples to illustrate this possibility.

Others are not so sure about the promise of e-democracy. Some recognise that there is a lot of political activity online but believe there will be little change 'on the ground' – politics as usual will continue (Graber et al., 2004). Some refer to the *digital divide* – the divide between rich and poor in access to the Internet. This may well increase rather than reduce social inequalities. And even if access to the Internet is widened, this is unlikely to solve major social problems such as overcoming world poverty (Norris, 2001).

activity8 e-democracy

Item A   *Blogs in Iran*

An Iranian blog in English

Blog is short for weblog. A weblog is an online journal, newsletter or diary which is regularly updated. Usually created by individuals, blogs deal with a vast range of topics from politics and social issues to music and celebrities.

In the last five years, the Iranian judiciary have closed down around 100 publications, including 41 daily newspapers. The mullahs – religious leaders – impose strict rules on dress and behaviour and censor media output in line with their views on religious correctness. In the absence of freedom of speech, an estimated 75,000 Iranians have turned to weblogs. Farsi, the main language of Iran is now the 4th most popular language for online journals. Blogs provide people with anonymity and freedom of expression. They allow people to criticise the government and to indulge their tastes for things banned by the regime – from Harry Potter to Marilyn Manson.

Adapted from *guardian.co.uk* , 2005

Item B Riots in France

Riots in Toulouse, France

Both the government and the rioters used the Internet during the riots in French towns and cities in November, 2005. Three young bloggers were arrested for urging people to burn down their nearest police station. The interior minister, Nicolas Sarkozy took out ads on Google to broadcast the government's point of view. A few years ago, he would have held a press conference – now he speaks through a search engine.

Adapted from *Jarvis*, 2005

Item C The Zapatistas

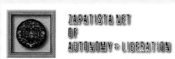

The Zapatistas are a revolutionary movement in Chiapas, a state in southern Mexico. They have formed a grass-roots movement for self-government – in their words, for 'autonomy, justice and freedom'. They have an extensive website and make widespread use of the Internet to organise their movement and gain international support. They invite visitors to their website to express their own views and participate in the movement. They see their struggle in part as a 'cyberwar' – a battle for hearts and minds in cyberspace. In their words, 'The revolution will be digitised'.

Adapted from *Zapatista Net of Autonomy & Liberation*, 2005

Zapatista leader, Subcommander Marcos

Item D The anti-capitalist movement - organisation

Some of the thousands of demonstrators protesting against the World Trade Organisation (WTO), Seattle, 30 November, 1999. They see the WTO as an organisation for global capitalism.

An anti-capitalist activist, Anne, says 'We are totally interconnected, like a big family'.

Websites play a key role in bringing so many people together. But activists say it is e-mail which has really revolutionised the movement. You can start with a very small distribution list, but then as everyone on their own personal mail list forwards a message to everyone on their own personal mail list, it cascades down to an enormous number of people. This makes it almost impossible for the police to estimate the level of any threat, or to guess at the number involved.

Adapted from *Reeves*, 1999

Item E Impact of the anti-capitalist movement

It was the appearance of the anti-capitalist demonstrators in Seattle in November 1999 that first made business leaders take notice of their concerns. Company chairmen forced to cower behind police lines cannot help but be impressed by the strength of feeling and the powers of organisation of people who might be ignored if they contented themselves with polite protest. The force of the attack has been strengthened because it has penetrated the system. Socially responsible investors, such as those putting pressure on BP and other oil companies, bring the arguments to the boardroom.

One response has been a drive within business for greater responsibility and openness. For example, the EU has backed a new organisation, CSR Europe, which was behind the European Parliament's first conference on corporate responsibility. Self-interest is a significant driver of this growing concern. For example, companies with strong brands (such as Nike and Adidas) have realised they must protect their reputations. That means, among other things, trying to ensure suppliers do not employ children or pay low wages.

Adapted from *Cowe*, 2001

Item F The digital divide

Global internet use (in millions)

	1998	1999	2000	2002
World Total	149.75	201.00	407.00	605.60
Africa	0.80	1.72	3.11	6.31
Asia/Pacific	25.92	33.61	104.88	187.24
Europe	30.86	47.15	113.14	190.91
Middle-East	0.78	0.88	2.40	5.12
Canada & USA	87.00	112.4	167.12	182.67
South America	4.50	5.29	16.45	33.35

Source: *NUA Internet Surveys*

questions

1 What evidence is provided by Items A to E which suggests that:

a) e-democracy is working

b) e-democracy is leading to change 'on the ground'?

2 What does Item F say to those who are optimistic about the future of e-democracy?

The Internet: media giants and global inequality Not all commentators are so optimistic about the potential of the Internet to aid freedom and democracy. They point to the domination of the Internet by a small number of huge corporations and to global inequality of access to the Internet.

The Internet is dominated by a few major media organisations. Microsoft is the best known. It not only developed the software for personal computers that was essential for the widespread take-up of the Internet, but has also become a major Internet service provider (ISP). A few transnational companies, including the biggest media organisation, America Online (AOL) Time Warner, own and control the most widely used Internet service providers. These ISPs enable us to log on in the first place, direct users to particular commercial services and play a key role in online advertising. Since the mid-1990s, the Internet has become much more commercialised. E-commerce has taken off and there has been 'a shift from educational to commercial use' (Gorman & McLean, 2003).

There is considerable inequality in Internet access. Castells (1996) argues that Internet use remains 'the domain of an educated segment of the population of the most advanced societies'. In many countries, the technology needed for widespread Internet use is undeveloped, and in other countries people do not have the income or skills to use the Internet.

The Internet and e-commerce E-commerce is here to stay. For example, Amazon, which began as an online bookseller and moved into DVDs, CDs, electrical goods and white goods (washing machines, fridges), goes from strength to strength. And every major company has its own website from which it advertises and often sells its goods and services.

Some see e-commerce as a positive development. It offers more choice to consumers, it increases competition, it often leads to lower prices and it puts consumers in control – they can compare prices and pick and choose from a vast range of products. Others see the development of e-commerce in a negative light. It encourages materialism and consumerism and furthers capitalist domination and control.

Evaluation

The freedom and lack of regulation of the Internet is both its strength and its weakness.

On the positive side, a vast range of information is available and a wide variety of views can be heard. Public debate can take place across the world.

On the negative side, lack of control of the Internet means that information can be inaccurate, one-sided or simply not true. Extreme views (racist, sexist, homophobic and political) are freely available.

Some people have called for greater regulation of the Internet by governments. At present, information can only be controlled if it breaks the laws of a particular country – for example, the clamp down on use of the Internet by paedophiles. Others believe that irresponsible use of the Internet is a price worth paying for the free expression and exchange of information it provides.

key terms

E-commerce Commercial activities conducted on the Internet, eg advertising and selling goods and services.

E-democracy Democratic activities conducted on the Internet, eg the free and uncensored presentation and discussion of issues people see as important to them as citizens.

Digitalisation The translation of information – images, texts and sounds – into a universal computer language.

Public sphere A space where people can freely debate issues which are important to them as citizens.

Digital divide Divisions between different groups in access to the Internet, eg between rich and poor.

*activity*9 *e-commerce*

Item A *Amazon.com*

Item B *BMW*

Welcome to BMW.

Welcome to the Hottest Internet link for the Wildest Uncensored Erotic Adult Pleasures!

Millions of men log on to adult sex sites every day. One estimate puts their annual revenue at £70-100 million.
(Observer, 30.3.2003)

Item C *Sex.com*

In 1994, a young computer engineer registered the domain name 'sex.com'. Now, after a decade of legal battles, he has finally won the right to regain control of the world's most valuable web address.

Gary Kremen realised the potential of the Internet in 1994 and applied for the domain 'sex.com'. At the time, the Internet was only known to academics and computer students. Kremen couldn't believe it when he was awarded – for free – a piece of Internet property now worth $500,000 a month just in advertising space.

Adapted from *The Guardian*, 26.6.2003

question

Discuss the different views on e-commerce with some reference to the above items.

summary

1. From a pluralist view, media content mirrors what the public, or a section of the public wants. In other words, the media simply respond to the demands of the market.

2. If media organisations did not reflect public demand, they would go out of business.

3. In general, pluralists welcome media deregulation, seeing it as offering diversity and choice. They argue that privately-owned media organisations, in competition with each other, are the most effective way of providing choice.

4. Critics of the pluralist view argue that media concentration is a threat to democracy. Media content is seen to reflect the views of media owners and advertisers – the views broadcast are increasingly conservative with little room for liberal or radical voices. Privately-owned media organisations are in business to make money rather than to provide a public service.

5. Owners may influence the content of the mass media directly by using the media to put their own views across. They also exert an indirect influence by setting the goals of the organisation and making key financial decisions.

6. Marxist theories see the media as an instrument of ideological domination. Media content reflects the interests of the powerful and controls the thinking of the population.

7. Neo-Marxists argue that cultural hegemony is never complete, never totally dominant. There are always ideas and beliefs which challenge cultural hegemony.

8. The term ideology has been used in a number of ways. Marxists and feminists use it in a negative sense. For them, ideology is a distortion of reality which justifies inequality. There are also a number of neutral views which see ideology as a set of ideas and values which direct political action. Used in this way, ideology is not good or bad, true or false.

9. Technological developments are creating new media. These include cable television, satellite broadcasting, and the Internet.

10. Some argue that the new media increase diversity and choice. Others argue that satellite and cable broadcasting simply produce more of the same and often lead to a reduction in the quality of media content.

11. Some see the Internet revitalising democracy – it allows people to freely express their views and directly participate in the democratic process. Others are not so sure about the promise of e-democracy. They question the view that online political activity will lead to real change 'on the ground'.

12. Some see e-commerce as a positive development – offering more choice to consumers, lowering prices and putting consumers in control. Others see it in a negative light – encouraging materialism and consumerism and furthering capitalist domination.

Unit 3 Selection and presentation of media content

keyissues

1 How is news constructed?

2 What are moral panics and how do they arise?

3.1 The construction of news

This unit looks at the selection and presentation of media content using the reporting of news as an example. Williams (2003) identifies three important influences on media content.

● The power of those who actually work in the media – people like journalists

● The day-to-day organisation and routine of media companies

● The culture of society – its wider norms and values.

We shall examine each of these factors by taking a specific example: the production of news.

The influence of media workers

An influential study conducted by White in 1950 argued that particular individuals play a significant role in determining which items make news. This study was based on the decisions made by one news editor on what should appear as national and international news in a small American newspaper. White's study suggested that the editor's individual prejudices played a significant role in the selection process. He acted as a *gatekeeper,* only allowing his preferred stories to pass through the 'gate' into the news.

Later research has challenged this view. An investigation of the selections made by a number of news editors did not find any significant variation in the news items they chose (Williams, 2003). This suggests that individual media workers are influenced in their decision-making by the organisations in which they work rather than their own preferences. Such a suggestion is reinforced when we realise that the selection of news involves many people – no one individual can be held responsible for the final product.

The influence of organisational structures

Watch the 10 o'clock news on ITV and BBC. While there is some variation in the events reported, there is also a noticeable similarity between the two news broadcasts on any day. This agreement over what counts as 'news' is the starting point for sociologists who highlight the importance of organisational structures in shaping the news. They believe that the routines of news organisations and the occupational socialisation of journalists are vital in explaining the content of the news.

Routines A daily newspaper works on a 24 hour cycle. To ensure that the news is fresh, one routine adopted is to focus on events that occur within that cycle. A train crash occurring since the previous day's newspaper is more likely to be reported as news than a famine that unfolds over time.

To make the reporting of events manageable, newspapers are divided up into sections (foreign news, crime news, sports news etc) and specialist correspondents are allocated to report on different kinds of news. Events happening in the real world are squeezed into these sections, with those occurring in locations where journalists are placed the most likely to be reported. So we know more about what is happening in North America and Europe than in South America and Africa.

News values Journalists learn the kind of events seen as newsworthy in the course of their professional socialisation. They pick up a set of informal rules or *news values* which enable them to identify what is newsworthy. A former editor of *The Guardian* identifies these news values as follows:

Significance: social, economic, political, human.

Drama: the excitement, action and entertainment in the event.

Surprise: the freshness, newness, unpredictability.

Personalities: royal, political, 'showbiz', others.

Sex, scandal, crime: popular ingredients.

Numbers: the scale of the event, numbers of people affected.

Proximity: on our doorsteps, or 10,000 miles away?

(Hetherington, 1985).

Events that correspond to these values are more likely to be identified as newsworthy than others. What's more, in reporting these events, journalists will present them in dramatic and personalised terms. 'Surprises' become 'shocks'; 'disagreements' become 'open conflicts'; and political debates are translated into choices between rival personalities (McCullagh, 2002).

News values have to be interpreted on a daily basis, with newspapers differing in the priority they give to some news values over others. However, there is often a remarkable similarity across the British news media when it comes to the main story of the day (Allan, 1999).

Objectivity Journalists often claim to be objective – to provide balanced and neutral accounts of events. Tuchman (1978) argues that the desire for objectivity means that the news media adopt a number of conventions in reporting the news. Facts are distinguished from opinions, with hard news, for example, being separated from editorial comment. The most important elements of the story are presented first, with the background outlined later. Different sides of the story are given; supporting evidence is produced for the claims made; and reliable sources are quoted.

However, in practice, these conventions mean that the voices of powerful organisations such as the government are often given prominence as they tend to be seen by the media as credible and authoritative.

Frameworks To enable newsworthy events to be understood by audiences, the news media place them within familiar frameworks. Take the coverage of two seemingly similar tragedies, the shooting down of a Korean civilian airliner by the Soviet Union in 1983 and the shooting down of an Iranian airbus by the USA in 1986. Both events took place during the 'cold war' when communism was seen as a threat to Western societies. In this context, a common way of interpreting events involved a contrast between the civilised West and the uncivilised East. In both the American and British news media, this familiar framework was employed to interpret what happened in 1983 and 1986. The first event was presented as 'a barbaric, terrorist, heinous act', while the second was presented as 'an understandable accident' (McNair, 1996).

This framework was of course not the only one that could have been used. The Soviet (Russian communist) news media reversed the Western view and interpreted the first event as an unfortunate accident and the second as a terrorist act.

In Britain and America the same framework was used across the news media and reflected how both governments saw these incidents. Hall et al., (1978) argue that this is not uncommon and that powerful groups are able to act as *primary definers*. Less powerful voices may be heard, but these voices are often drowned out. And when they are not drowned out, they are often ridiculed.

Evaluation Sociologists agree that we need to take account of the influence of both media owners and organisational factors in order to understand the production of media messages. In many cases, these influences mean that media coverage reflects the interests of powerful groups. However, this is not always the case.

Powerful groups do not always speak with one voice. This means that there can be conflict over how events are to be interpreted. Powerful groups disagreed about war with Iraq in 2003. And they are bitterly divided over Britain's adoption of the euro as its currency. In these instances, it is not possible to identify one primary definition of the issues.

The media sometimes challenge powerful groups. Some investigative journalists can become the primary definers, with powerful groups being obliged to respond to the way

*activity*10 *news values*

Item A *Islanders consider exodus as sea levels rise*

Tuvaluan children playing in the sea which threatens to swamp their island.

Faced with the prospect of being swamped by rising sea levels, the Pacific island nation of Tuvalu is considering evacuating its 9,300 residents.

With sea levels predicted to rise by more than 80 cms over the next century due to global warming, Tuvaluans are living on borrowed time. The most recent figures suggest that Tuvalu's sea levels have risen nearly three times as fast as the world average over the past decade, and are now 5cms higher than in 1993.

Adapted from *The Guardian*, 19.7.2003

Item B *Harry is 'out of control'*

Prince Harry's late-night drinking and wild behaviour have forced one of his royal protection officers to quit. Sergeant Ieuan Jones was transferred to other duties after telling colleagues he could not cope with the tearaway Prince.

One Buckingham Palace worker said: 'He won't do what he is told and when you are dealing with the safety of someone like him that is a dangerous situation. They get totally fed up sitting around in pub after pub while Harry knocks back drink after drink. They can only have tonic water or coke and it gets very boring indeed for them.'

Adapted from *Sunday Express*, 20.7.2003

Item C A balanced discussion

"AND TO ENSURE A BALANCED AND IMPARTIAL DISCUSSION OF THE LATEST GOVERNMENT MEASURES, I HAVE WITH ME A GOVERNMENT SPOKESMAN AND A WILD-EYED MILITANT FROM THE LUNATIC FRINGE."

Adapted from *Glasgow Media Group*, 1982

Item D Reporting the intifada

The Glasgow Media Group analysed coverage of the Palestinian intifada (uprising) in 89 TV news bulletins broadcast by BBC1 and ITV in 2000. They found important differences in the language used to describe Israeli and Palestinian deaths. When Israelis were killed, words such as 'murder', 'atrocity', 'lynching' and 'savage cold-blooded killing' were used. But when Palestinians died at Israeli hands, the language used was considerably more moderate.

Adapted from Philo & Miller, 2002

questions

1 Assess the 'newsworthiness' of the news stories in Items A and B using the list of news values.

2 What point is being made by the cartoon in Item C? What does it suggest about the influence of the powerful?

3 What does Item D suggest about the claim that TV news is objective?

---

the media define the issues. Two journalists on the *Washington Post,* for example, uncovered a range of illegal activities by the US government that culminated in the resignation of the President in 1974 (Schlesinger,1991). And in 2005, the *Washington Post* revealed the existence of a network of detention centres in eastern Europe set up by the United States to interrogate suspected terrorists.

The influence of wider culture

What counts as news and the way it is reported will, to some extent, reflect the wider culture – the shared norms, values, concerns and beliefs of society. To take an obvious example, baseball, ice hockey, basketball and American football dominate sports reporting in newspapers in the USA. They are rarely found in British newspapers.

News often reflects strongly held values. For example, murder is regularly reported and condemned. This reflects the high value placed on human life.

News reporting often draws on widely held cultural stereotypes. For example, Schudson (2000) argues that news reports which represent young Black people as a problem and women as sex objects reflect shared cultural stereotypes.

We live in an age where organisations attempt to manage the news, to 'spin' information in order to present themselves in the best possible light. They try to ensure that their actions are seen to be in line with society's norms and values. For example, Tony Blair's Labour government has been accused of exaggerating the threat of weapons of mass destruction in order to justify the war against Iraq and the deaths of British soldiers and Iraqi civilians.

However, governments and powerful organisations are not always able to portray their actions as fitting the norms and values of society. For example, it is difficult for governments and business organisations to control media coverage when accidents such as oil spills and explosions at nuclear plants occur (McCullagh, 2002).

Conclusion

Most researchers see the construction of news in the following way. Here's how Graeme Burton (2005) summarises the process of news creation.

- News is socially constructed – it is created within a framework of social relationships and cultural beliefs.
- There is no 'truth out there' which is reported in the news.
- News consists of information that is selected and interpreted on the basis of national norms, values and concerns.
- Those who actually construct the news – editors and journalists – do so within organisational structures and in terms of news values. These structures and values define what counts as news.

key terms

Gatekeeping Making decisions about what will and will not become 'news'.

News values A set of informal rules used by journalists to identify what is newsworthy.

Primary definers Individuals and groups who are able to influence what events become news and how they are reported.

activity11 news frameworks

The Gulf War (1990-91) was fought between Iraq, led by Saddam Hussein, and the Allies (USA, Britain and a number of other countries) led by the American president George Bush Sr. The table below shows some of the words and phrases used by the British media to describe each side.

Mad dogs and Englishmen	
We have	**They have**
Army, Navy and Air Force	A war machine
Reporting guidelines	Censorship
Press briefings	Propaganda
We	**They**
Take out	Destroy
Suppress	Destroy
Eliminate	Kill
Neutralise	Kill
Dig in	Cower in their foxholes
We Launch	**They Launch**
First strikes	Sneak missile attacks
Pre-emptively	Without provocation
Our boys are...	**Theirs are...**
Professional	Brainwashed
Lion-hearts	Paper tigers
Cautious	Cowardly
Confident	Desperate
Heroes	Cornered
Dare-devils	Cannon fodder
Young knights of the skies	Bastards of Baghdad
Loyal	Blindly obedient
Desert rats	Mad dogs
Resolute	Ruthless
Brave	Fanatical

Adapted from *The Guardian*, 23.1.1991

questions

1 What framework is the British news media using?

2 The Iraqi news media was tightly controlled by Saddam Hussein's regime.

  a) What framework might they use?

  b) Suggest two phrases they might use to describe the Allies.

3.2 The news and moral panics

Journalists often claim that the news represents a 'mirror on the world' (Allan, 1999). They believe that the news gives an accurate and impartial reflection of events. Research evidence gives a somewhat different picture. Section 3.1 showed that the news media not only select certain events as newsworthy, but also place a particular interpretation on those events. From this point of view, the media construct news rather than mirror the world.

Mods and rockers It is not unusual for the news media – especially the tabloid press – to sensationalise the events they report. This can be seen from the following research. In a groundbreaking study conducted in the 1960s, Stanley Cohen looked at media coverage of the activities of two youth subcultures – mods and rockers. On Easter bank holiday in 1964, large numbers of young people, including mods on their scooters and rockers on their motor cycles, went to Clacton for a day out at the seaside. Cohen was interested in how the media reported their behaviour and the consequences of that reporting.

The media presented a picture of two rival gangs 'hell bent on destruction'. Fighting, vandalism and anti-social behaviour were reported as widespread and those responsible were identified as mods and rockers.

On closer inspection, Cohen found little evidence of serious violence and vandalism. True, there were large crowds of often noisy young people. And there were mods and rockers baiting each other and sometimes getting into scuffles. But most young people did not identify with either group, and were not involved in any disturbances.

The mass media had presented a distorted and sensationalised picture of events. And this media picture created public fears and concerns about mods and rockers. The police responded to these concerns by increasing their presence at seaside resorts on future bank holidays and by making more and more arrests. Young people resented what they saw as heavy-handed and unjustified police behaviour and were more likely to identify with mods and rockers. There were further disturbances followed by yet more sensationalised reporting, and increased police activity in response to public demands to deal with the 'problem'.

Moral panics Cohen argued that the reaction of the media created what he called a *moral panic*. A moral panic exists when 'a condition, episode, person or group of persons emerges to become defined as a threat to societal values and interests' (Cohen, 1987). In this particular case, mods and rockers were singled out as *folk devils* whose behaviour was seen as a threat to social order.

Creating a moral panic Moral panics occur on a regular basis. Newspapers (especially tabloid newspapers) often play a key role in their creation. They sensationalise issues by using emotive headlines, language and pictures. They present groups as stereotypes. They associate those groups with stereotypical behaviour – for example, New Age Travellers with drugs; Black youth with street crime; English football supporters abroad with violence. Contrasts are drawn between a rosy image of the past and a decline in modern-day morals. Finally, the media clamour for a clampdown on the group, and/or the behaviour identified as a threat.

Young people and moral panics Young people continue to be the focus of moral panics. Their behaviour has frequently been identified as a problem. Examples include youth subcultures such as hippies, skinheads and punks, and behaviour associated with young people such as street crime, football hooliganism and drug taking.

Young people are sometimes seen as the victims in moral panics. Critcher (2003) argues that moral panics increasingly focus on threats to children. Concern over child abuse, paedophilia and the influence of violent films on young viewers are examples of these kinds of moral panics.

Features of a moral panic The term moral panic has been taken up widely and is now regularly used by politicians and journalists. Often the term is used quite loosely. Goode and Ben-Yehuda (1994) try to define moral panic precisely. They argue that moral panics have five distinguishing features.

- Increased public concern over the behaviour of a certain group
- Increased hostility towards the group
- A certain level of public agreement that there is a real threat and that it is caused by the group
- Public concern is out of proportion to the real harm caused by the group
- Moral panics appear and disappear very quickly. (Goode & Ben-Yehuda, 1994)

*activity*12 *paedophilia: a moral panic?*

Item A Tabloid headline

WE TRAP INTERNET CHILD SEX SICKO

Shocking Internet peril that all concerned parents should be aware of

Adapted from *The People*, 20.7.2003

Mothers of four murdered children lead a march through central London demanding more action to protect youngsters from paedophiles.

question

With reference to the items, explain how media concern over paedophilia can be described as a moral panic.

Item B Public reaction

Eight-year-old Sarah Payne was abducted while playing near her grandparents' house in West Sussex on July 1st 2000. Her half-buried body was found by a farm labourer on July 17th. On December 12th 2001, a 42-year-old local man and convicted sex offender, Roy Whiting, was found guilty of her 'sexually-motivated' murder and sentenced to life imprisonment.

When Sarah Payne's body was discovered, the *News of the World* launched a campaign: How do you know if there's a paedophile in your midst? The paper published the names and photographs of 50 people it claimed had committed child sex offences, and promised: 'We pledge we will pursue our campaign until we have publicly named and shamed every paedophile in Britain'.

The paper produced figures suggesting 88% of Britons believed parents should be told if a child sex offender was living in their area. It provided a website on which parents could use an interactive map to find their local paedophiles. It asked readers to report any convicted child abusers living in their area. And it published an endorsement of the campaign from Sarah's parents, Sarah and Michael Payne, who later spoke of their unease at being press-ganged into giving the campaign their support.

From Plymouth to Portsmouth, Manchester to London, wrongly identified men and known paedophiles found themselves being hounded by mobs up to 300 strong. The vigilante action was most severe on the Paulsgrove estate in Portsmouth, where protesters circulated a list of 20 alleged sex offenders in the community and proceeded to target them.

The crowds – 40 of whom were later charged with offences – smashed windows, torched cars and forced five families, wrongly identified as harbouring sex offenders, out of their homes. A suspected paedophile in nearby Southampton shot himself dead and a female registrar was hounded from her South Wales home because neighbours confused 'paediatrician' with 'paedophile.'

Adapted from *The Guardian*, 13.12.2001

Evaluation Critcher (2003) examined five case studies – Aids, ecstasy and raves, video 'nasties', child abuse in families, and paedophilia. In his view, only two of these cases were full moral panics – video 'nasties' and paedophilia. In these cases an issue was seen as a threat; the media defined the 'problem' in the same way; organised groups generally supported the panic; and the state eventually responded by bringing in new legislation to combat the apparent threat.

Critcher challenges the view that moral panics are always triggered by a concern over identifiable folk devils. What triggered concern in the cases he examined was the death of children or young people. These events were seen to reflect major social problems. In only one of the cases was there an indisputable folk devil – the paedophile.

Critcher argues that a consensus (agreement) is necessary for a moral panic to develop. Some newspapers

activity 13 video 'nasties'

Item A The Video Recording Bill

The Video Recording Bill was passed by the Conservative government in 1984. Its aim was to place strict controls on video 'nasties' – videos with high levels of violence and sex which were seen as harmful to children.

Adapted from Harris, 1984

Item B Child's Play

In November 1993, two 11-year-old boys from Merseyside were found guilty of murdering a two-year-old child. The 'horror' video *Child's Play 3* had been rented by the father of one of the boys shortly before the murder. There were certain similarities between scenes in the video and the killing of the child. But there was no evidence that either boy had seen the video. Despite this, the judge at the trial stated, 'I suspect that exposure to violent films may in part be an explanation'.

Adapted from *The Guardian*, 26.11.1993

Item C The police view

Merseyside police detectives who had interviewed the boys for several weeks before the trial rejected any suggestions that 'horror' videos had influenced the boys' behaviour. One detective said, 'I don't know where the judge got that idea from. I couldn't believe it when I heard him. We went through something like 200 titles rented by the family. There were some you or I wouldn't want to see, but nothing – no scene, or plot, or dialogue – where you could put your finger on the freeze button and say that influenced a boy to go out and commit murder.'

Quoted in *The Independent*, 26.11.1993

Item D Reaction in Parliament

In the Commons, the Conservative MP Sir Ivan Lawrence QC called for action to curb 'the constant diet of violence and depravity' fed to youngsters through television, videos and computer pornography. Sir Ivan, chairman of the Home Affairs Select Committee, said it was becoming 'daily more obvious' that this was a major reason for the rise in juvenile crime.

Quoted in *The Independent*, 26.11.1993

Item E Burning videos

Azad Video, Scotland's largest video renting chain, burned its *Child's Play* videos including 300 copies of *Child's Play 3*. Xtra-Vision, the Irish Republic's biggest video chain, withdrew *Child's Play* from its shelves.

Adapted from *The Sun*, 26.11.93

Item F The Sun's reaction

The Sun, 26.11.1993

Item G Moral panics

At the turn of the century, there was great concern about violent images in Penny Dreadful comics. In the 1950s, panic that horror comics would lead to children copying the things they saw, led to the Children and Young Persons (Harmful Publications) Act 1955. In the 1980s, there was the huge panic about films such as *Drillerkiller*, which also led to a new law. There's been a recurrent moral panic about violent images which looks to a mythical golden age of tranquil behaviour.

T. Newburn, Policy Studies Institute, quoted in *The Guardian*, 26.11.1993

Item H Press editorials, 26.11.1993

The uncanny resemblance between the film *Child's Play 3* and the murder must be of concern. A link between the film and the crime would not prove that the former caused the latter. Yet it seems quite possible that exposure to images of brutality could turn an already disturbed child towards violence.

(Independent)

More and more children are growing up in a moral vacuum, which for so many is being filled with fetid (stinking) junk from the lower depths of our popular culture – video nasties, crude comics and violent television.

(Daily Express)

Instead of urging legislation to ban violent films, it would surely be more to the point if we took it upon ourselves as adults to ensure their prohibition in our own homes.

(Daily Telegraph)

questions

1 Read Items A, B, C and D. What justification is there for the views of the judge and Ivan Lawrence? Why do you think they reacted in this way?

2 Do you think the reactions in Items B, D, E, F and H can be described as a moral panic? With some reference to Item G, give reasons for your answer.

tried to create a moral panic over Aids by identifying it as 'a gay plague'. They were unsuccessful because experts challenged this view and Aids was eventually seen as a health risk to the population as a whole.

Critcher disagrees with the last feature of moral panics identified by Goode and Ben-Yehuda – that they appear and disappear very quickly. He gives examples of moral panics that last for years.

For instance, a moral panic over drugs has continued over the past 40 years. And even when a moral panic ends, it often comes back. For example, there was a moral panic over video nasties from 1982-1984. It re-appeared in 1993, as Activity 13 shows.

key terms

Moral panic Widespread public concern, usually fuelled by sensational media coverage, that an event or group is threatening society.

Folk devils Groups whose behaviour is seen as a threat to social order.

summary

1. The production of media content is influenced by professionals such as editors and journalists.

2. The work of professionals in the news media is influenced by organisational factors such as the routines of news reporting and by ideas about what is newsworthy (news values).

3. The wider cultural environment also influences media content. Powerful organisations usually have the ability to become primary definers of the news. And journalists are influenced by dominant cultural values and assumptions.

4. The mass media select certain events as newsworthy and place a particular interpretation on those events. In this way, the media construct news rather than mirror the world.

5. At times, the media sensationalise the events they report. This can lead to moral panics.

6. Certain groups of young people are seen as a threat to social order and a cause for public concern. Sensationalised reporting of their activities can result in a moral panic.

7. Moral panics sometimes view young people as victims – for example, as victims of paedophiles.

Unit 4 Media representations

keyissues

1 What are representations?

2 How do the media represent different social groups?

4.1 Representations and stereotypes

Representations We experience many events first hand. We meet other people, go to school or college, visit different areas and so on. The judgements we make about these people, events and places are based on our own direct impressions.

However, we directly experience only a tiny proportion of the world. We rely on the media for knowledge about unfamiliar places, people and events. The sort of information we gain from the media is indirect – the media actually re-present the world to us. In providing these *representations* of the world, the media will highlight some aspects and neglect others. The language they use and the pictures they choose will give particular impressions.

In general, the media do not have very long to provide background detail. For example, news broadcasts are made up of a number of short items. This means that 'shorthand' methods are often used to describe people and events. The media tend to rely on the images of particular groups that are already in the heads of their audience. In other words, they rely on *stereotypes*.

Stereotypes The term stereotype was introduced by the journalist Walter Lippman in his book *Public Opinion*, published in 1922. He described stereotypes as 'the little pictures we carry around in our heads'. Stereotypes are widely-held beliefs about the characteristics of members of social groups. Simply because they belong to a particular group, people are seen to have certain attitudes and behaviour.

Stereotypes are generalisations – they are applied to all members of a group. For example, Germans may be seen as efficient, Black people as good athletes and students as layabouts. Stereotypes can be positive or negative, they can offer a favourable or unfavourable image of a group. Nurses are usually pictured as kind and caring, whereas dealers in stocks and shares are often portrayed as money-grabbing and selfish.

Representations of social groups Representations are important because we depend on the media for much of our information about society. Even when we have direct experience of different social groups, media representations will still be in our heads. This will affect the way we think about and interact with others.

This unit looks at representations of gender, ethnicity, social class, age, sexuality and disability.

activity14 stereotyping

Item A Racial stereotypes

A number of experiments were conducted in the USA using the following procedure. After being shown this picture, one participant described it to a second participant, who then described it to a third, and so on. After six descriptions, over half the final participants reported that the Black person, not the White person, was holding the razor. Some even had the Black person waving the razor in a threatening manner.

Adapted from Allport & Postman, 1947

Item B American stereotypes of Japanese

1932	1950	1967
intelligent	treacherous	industrious
industrious	sly	ambitious
progressive	extremely nationalistic	efficient

Adapted from Katz & Braly, 1933; Gilbert, 1951; Karlins, Coffman & Walters, 1969

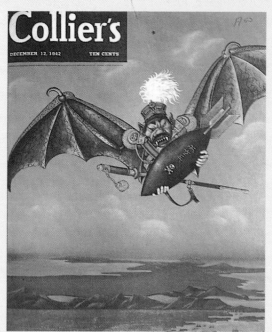

The cover of an American magazine published five days after the Japanese bombed the American fleet at Pearl Harbour in 1941.

A response by an American cartoonist to the torture and execution of American airmen who had bailed out from damaged planes during a bombing raid over Japan. (Tojo was the Japanese Prime Minister during World War II.)

questions

1 Explain the results of the experiment in Item A, using the idea of stereotypes.

2 Look at Item B.

   a) Describe the changes in American stereotypes of Japanese.

   b) Suggest reasons for these changes.

4.2 Representations of gender

Gender stereotypes: the 1950s to 1970s What is a woman? Judging from media representations of women from the 1950s to the 1970s, a woman is a:

- housewife and mother
- domestic servant
- domestic consumer
- sex object.

This stereotypical view of women was particularly apparent in advertising where the roles of housewife, domestic servant and domestic consumer were often combined. For example, women were regularly presented as cleaners, consuming particular brands of washing powder, washing-up liquid, furniture polish, toilet cleansers, air fresheners, disinfectants and the like. At other times, they were presented as sex objects selling products to women to make them appear more attractive to men, or using their sex-appeal to sell products to men.

When the media portrayed women outside this narrow stereotype, it was often in negative terms. A study of gender representations in the American media from the 1950s to the 1970s found that women shown in paid employment on TV programmes often had unstable or unsatisfactory relationships with male partners. Married women with jobs, particularly more demanding, higher-status jobs, were much more likely than full-time housewives to be portrayed as unhappily married in television drama and comedy (Tuchman, 1981).

The following quotation by Tunstall (1983) provides a summary of the main findings of research into gender representation in the media from the 1960s and 70s.

'The presentation of women in the media is biased because it emphasises women's domestic, sexual, consumer and marital activities to the exclusion of all else. Women are depicted as busy housewives, as contented mothers, as eager consumers and as sex objects. This does indeed indicate bias because, although similar numbers of men are fathers and husbands, the media has much less to say about these male roles. Just as men's domestic and marital roles are ignored, the media also ignore that well over half of British adult women go out to paid employment, and that many of both their interests and problems are employment-related' (Tunstall, 1983).

Patriarchy From a feminist perspective, the gender representations outlined above are an aspect of patriarchy – a social system based on male domination. Women are portrayed either as domestic servants providing comfort and support for men, or as sex objects to service men's sexual needs. In both cases, women play subordinate and subservient roles.

Such media representations suggest that these roles are natural and normal. Feminists see this as an example of patriarchal ideology – a set of beliefs which distorts reality and supports male dominance.

Changes in media representations of gender

There is some evidence that the representation of gender roles has become more equal and less stereotyped. Drawing upon two content analysis studies of gender representations on prime-time TV shows, Gauntlett (2002) identifies the following changes.

- A significant increase in the proportion of main female characters, from 18% in 1992-93, to 43% in 1995-96.
- A massive decrease since the 1970s in the proportion of women whose main occupation was represented as housewife – now only 3%.
- A marked shift towards equality within the last two decades. 'Female and male characters are likely to be as intelligent, talented and resourceful – or stupid – as each other' (Gauntlett, 2002).

Films, soaps and sit-coms

Further evidence that gender representations are changing comes from analysis of films, soap operas and situation comedies. Gauntlett (2002) argues that women and men tend to have similar skills and abilities in films today. While a film like *Charlie's Angels* does focus on women as physically attractive, they are also presented as 'amazingly multi-skilled'.

Strong female characters are central to British soap operas and many actually drive the stories, for example Peggy Mitchell of *EastEnders* (Abercrombie, 1996).

In situation comedies, women are no longer portrayed in traditional 'feminine' roles. For example, both *Roseanne*

activity 15 gender stereotypes

questions

1 What stereotypes are illustrated in these representations of women?

2 How can they be seen as examples of patriarchal ideology?

and *Absolutely Fabulous* show 'unruly women who refuse the straightjacket of femininity' (Newbold et al., 2002).

Women's magazines Evidence of changes in gender representations are also evident in magazines targeted at young women. Ferguson (1983) conducted a study of young women's magazines from 1949 to 1980 and found that they promoted a traditional idea of femininity. The dominant assumption was that girls should aspire to be beautiful in order to get a husband and once married should become home-makers and carers.

By contrast, the focus of magazines since the 1980s is on young women seeking to control their own lives rather than being dependent on men. There is now more emphasis on sexuality and less on romance. Articles such as 'The hottest sex you'll ever have' (*MORE!* May, 2003) illustrate this shift. The traditional idea of femininity is challenged, with women no longer portrayed as the weaker sex. Instead, young women are encouraged 'to be assertive,

confident, and supportive of each other' (McRobbie, 1999). In some ways, these magazines turn the tables on men by encouraging women to be sexual aggressors rather than sexual objects (Gauntlett, 2002).

Evaluation Are the changes in media representations of women as significant as the above studies suggest? Think about the following evidence. A study of gender representations on American TV in 1995-96 found that men took 63% of the speaking roles compared to women's 37% (Gauntlett, 2002). Research on television sports coverage reveals that sportswomen continue to be under-represented. What little coverage there is 'tends to sexualise, trivialise and devalue women's sporting accomplishments' (Newbold et al., 2002).

While accepting the above points, available evidence indicates that media representations of women are now less likely to rely on traditional stereotypes and less likely to portray women in a narrow range of subordinate roles.

activity 16 *changing representations of women*

Angelina Jolie as Lara Croft in Tomb Raider.

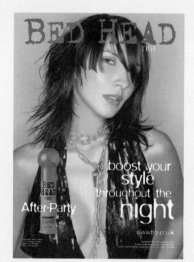

questions

1 How do the items illustrate changes in media representations of women?

2 To what extent do you think the items accurately represent media representation of women today?

4.3 Representations of ethnicity

Research into the media treatment of ethnicity has emphasised the way in which minority ethnic groups are almost always represented as a 'problem'. They tend to be reported as the cause of social disorder (eg, riots) and crime (eg, 'mugging'). While Black youths *are* involved in these actions, so are large numbers of White youths. The negative representation of minority ethnic groups was particularly noticeable in earlier decades, as the following example from the 1980s illustrates.

Racism and the press In a detailed examination of racism and the press, Van Dijk (1991) focused on the reporting of ethnic relations in the 1980s. He studied a sample of British newspapers from 1985 and 1989. His main finding was a positive presentation of White British citizens and a negative presentation of non-White British citizens. Minority group members were quoted less often and less fully than majority group members – even when minority 'experts' were available for comment. White authorities – especially the police and politicians – were the major speakers.

Van Dijk showed that the voice of the British press was predominantly 'white' in both 1985 and 1989, although some improvement was noticeable in the later sample.

Racial stereotypes Most recent studies argue that minority ethnic groups continue to be represented in a stereotypical way. The research, almost without exception, has emphasised the large proportion of negative images in the portrayal of Black and Asian people (Cottle, 2000). Complex differences – for example, those between different minority ethnic groups – are ignored. The point of view is virtually always a White one: that 'of the dominant looking at the subordinate: how *they* are different from us rather than how *we* are different from them' (Ross, 1996).

Overt and inferential racism Both press and television news are often seen by these studies as racist. However, there is a difference between what Hall (1995) calls 'overt' and 'inferential' racism. Overt racism is apparent when racist arguments are presented favourably. Sometimes overt racism does occur but more often what is at issue is inferential racism.

Inferential racism occurs when coverage seems balanced but is based on racist assumptions. Television news and current affairs programmes make an effort to be balanced yet debates are often based on the assumption that Black people are the 'source of the problem' (Hall, 1995).

Changes in media representations of ethnicity

Much of the research on racism and the media relates to the 1970s and early 1980s. In recent years there has been a growth in both the number and range of representations of minority ethnic groups.

Film and television drama and comedy In Britain the ideal of public service broadcasting has allowed Black programming to develop on Channel 4 and BBC2

(Daniels, 1996). This has led to the emergence of Black British cinema through films such as *My Beautiful Launderette* (Higson, 1998).

In recent years, programmes and films developed primarily for minority audiences have become popular with White audiences, for example, the Black sit-com, *Desmond's* and the Asian comedy, *Goodness Gracious Me*. Although integrated casting is still exceptional, Black and Asian actors 'are now playing "ordinary" characters...and the new way of presenting Black (and Asian) people effectively says to the audience that Black [and Asian] people are just like White people' (Abercrombie, 1996). This is apparent in popular programmes such as *The Bill* and *EastEnders* in Britain and *The Cosby Show* in America.

It is still rare for Black or Asian actors to receive star billing but even this has become more common. In some cases this has resulted in the production of positive images of minority communities as in the representation of the Black middle-class family the Huxtables in *The Cosby Show*. The overall result has been an expansion in 'the *range* of racial representations and the *complexity* of what it means to be Black [or Asian]' (Hall, 1997).

Advertising Changing representations are also evident in advertising. 'Colonial images and crudely nationalistic emblems are relatively rare in the current period' (Solomos & Back, 1996) and the under-representation of non-Whites in advertising is no longer evident (Glasgow Media Group, 1997). Instead, some multinational corporations now acknowledge and celebrate difference. A classic example is the 'United Colours of Benetton' advertising series in which the message of human unity is based on an acceptance of ethnic and cultural differences (see Activity 17, Item A). While this campaign and others have been criticised for reinforcing ethnic stereotypes, shifts towards a positive valuation of difference 'can unsettle...racism within popular culture' (Solomos & Back, 1996).

Even more unsettling to racist beliefs are the attempts by some artists to challenge our traditional ways of looking through the development of new forms of representation. An example is the presentation by Toscani, the photographer responsible for the Benetton campaign, of a series of well known people with transformed racial characteristics. The picture of the 'Black Queen', for example, reveals and challenges our taken-for-granted assumptions about the necessary whiteness of British identity (see Activity 17, Item C).

The news A study from the 1990s of news reporting on TV, radio and in newspapers presents an optimistic picture. The content analysis, conducted over a six month period from November 1996 to May 1997, revealed that most news items that dealt with racial issues put across an anti-racist message.

No explicit racist messages in cartoons could be found. Extensive coverage was given to instances of racism.

Immigration was treated in a sympathetic way and press silence on racist attacks was no longer evident. Multiculturalism and Islam were more likely to be valued than attacked. And minority voices were more likely to be heard.

However, the extent of progress should not be exaggerated. While deliberate bias against minorities was found to be rare, about a quarter of news items still conveyed a negative message about minority groups. And the old framework depicting minority ethnic groups as a social problem was at times all too evident, especially in the tabloid newspapers (Law, 1997).

Evaluation Research indicates that media representations of ethnicity do change. They are not simply based on the same old negative stereotypes. While old stereotypes do persist, for example in coverage of Islam after September 11th, media representations of ethnicity are becoming more diverse and more positive.

key terms

Representations The way the mass media portray particular social groups, individuals or events.

Stereotypes Widely held beliefs about the characteristics of members of social groups.

Content analysis A method of analysing the content of the mass media by counting the number of occurrences of particular words, phrases or images.

Patriarchal ideology The idea that traditional gender roles are natural and inevitable.

activity 17 changing representations of ethnicity

Item A Benetton ads

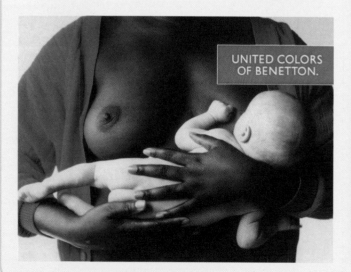

Item B Michael Jackson

Item C *Queen Elizabeth II*

Item D *Goodness, Gracious Me*

The following dialogue is from the comedy programme *Goodness, Gracious Me*.

The setting is late on a Friday night at an English restaurant in downtown Bombay. Several drunken Indians stagger in. A White waiter helps them into their seats.

I'm totally off my face. How come every Friday night we end up in a Berni Inn?

Cos that's what you do innit? You go out, you get tanked up and you go for an English.

They peer bleary-eyed at the menu.

Could I just have a chicken curry?

Oh no, Nina, it's an English restaurant, you've got to have something English – no spices.

But I don't like it, it's too bland.

Jam-mess (*mispronouncing James – the waiter*) What've you got that's not totally tasteless?

Steak and kidney pie sir?

There you are, steak and kidney pee.

No, no. It blocks me up. I won't go to the toilet for a week.

That's the whole point of having an English.

Adapted from Gillespie, 2002

question

How does each of the items demonstrate that media representations of ethnicity are changing?

4.4 Representations of social class

Media representations of social class have received less attention recently than those of gender and ethnicity. Research has focused primarily on representations of the working class.

Under-representation of the working class Many researchers note how rarely the average working person is represented in the media. 'Studies of 50 years of comic strips, radio serials, television dramas, movies and popular fiction reveal a very persistent pattern, an under-representation of working-class occupations and an over-representation of professional and managerial occupations among characters' (Butsch, 1995). And when it comes to the news, 'working-class people are likely to cross the screen only as witnesses to crimes or sports events, never as commentators or – even when their own lives are under discussion – as "experts"' (Ehrenreich, 1995).

The few representations there have been of the working class have consistently tended to be negative, as the following examples from situation comedies and the news illustrate.

Situation comedies and social class An American study of situation comedies over four decades from 1946 to 1990 showed that working-class males were typically represented as buffoons. 'They are dumb, immature, irresponsible or lacking in common sense. This is the character of the husbands in almost every sitcom depicting a blue-collar (White) male head of house, *The Honeymooners*, *The Flintstones*, *All in the Family* and *The Simpsons* being the most famous examples. He is typically well-intentioned, even loveable, but no one to respect or emulate. These men are placed against more mature, sensible wives'. In contrast, situation comedies featuring the middle class typically do not represent either parent as a buffoon but, where they do, it is the 'dizzy wife' as in *I Love Lucy*, with the husband here being portrayed as sensible and mature (Butsch, 1995).

The news and social class In Britain, the Glasgow Media Group have carried out a series of detailed studies of television news (Eldridge, 1995). They argue that the news is not impartial but reflects the interests of powerful groups. The coverage of industrial disputes – involving, for example, strikes of the Glasgow refuse collectors in the 1970s and miners in the 1980s – illustrates this.

- In terms of access to the media, management and the 'experts' receive far more coverage than trade unionists – in the Glasgow refuse strike for example, not one of the twenty-one interviews broadcast nationally was with a striker.

- Management and trade unionists are treated very differently. The former were usually allowed to make their points quietly and at length; the latter often had to shout over the noises around them or were interrupted by reporters.

The Glasgow Media Group conclude that the overall impression given by the media was that workers caused strikes and that 'excessive' wage demands caused inflation. What is in fact just one interpretation of the cause and effects of industrial disputes is presented as the dominant and authoritative one. This dominant view represents the working class in a negative way.

Even more negative is the depiction of the poor, many of whom are pictured as an underclass. One study showed that welfare issues only become newsworthy when associated with crime and fraud. By focusing on cases of welfare abuse, the media have portrayed the underclass as the undeserving poor, sponging off the welfare state (Golding & Middleton, 1982).

Soap operas and social class So far research has indicated that:

- the working class has typically been underrepresented in the media:

- when it has appeared, it has often been depicted in a negative manner.

British soap operas are something of an exception. Series such as *Coronation Street* and *EastEnders* feature the working class which continues to be represented as a close-knit community. While this community is portrayed as resilient, it is also increasingly depicted as multi-ethnic and threatened by outside criminal and racist forces (Dodd & Dodd, 1992).

Framing class

A recent American study based on a systematic content analysis of media representations of social class analysed the archives of major newspapers as well as 50 years of television entertainment programming (Kendall, 2005). It argues that the media selectively frame the world. 'A frame constitutes a storyline… about an issue' and this directs people's attention to some ideas rather than others. Surveying news stories and television entertainment across a range of media reveals a remarkable similarity in how events are framed. An example is the common coverage at Christmas of stories which feature charity towards the poor. 'These media representations suggest that Americans are benevolent people who do not forget the less fortunate' (Kendall, 2005).

Framing the rich and upper class In contemporary America, the upper class continues to be depicted generally in flattering terms. Kendall identifies four positive media frames.

- The consensus frame: the wealthy are like everyone else.

- The admiration frame: the wealthy are generous and caring people.

- The emulation frame: the wealthy personify the American Dream (anyone, whatever their origins, can be successful).

- The price-tag frame: the wealthy believe in the gospel of materialism.

While the above positive frames are dominant, two negative frames can also be distinguished.

- The sour grapes frame: the wealthy are unhappy and not well adjusted.

- The bad apple frame: some wealthy people are scoundrels.

Framing the poor and the working class In contrast to the generally sympathetic framing of the wealthy, 'much media coverage offers negative images of the poor, showing them as dependent on others (welfare issues) or as deviant in their behaviour and lifestyle'. Two common frames can be detected.

- The exceptionalism frame: if this person escaped poverty, why can't you?

- The charitable frame: the poor need a helping hand on special occasions like Christmas.

While the charitable frame exhibits some sympathy for the poor, it is very unusual to find any coverage that suggests the need to address the structural causes of poverty.

The working class is typically distinguished from the poor in America. This class also, is usually represented in a negative way.

- The shady frame: greedy workers, union disputes and organised crime.

- The caricature frame: rednecks, buffoons, bigots & slobs.

- The fading blue-collar frame: out of work or unhappy at work.

Occasionally a more positive frame can be detected.

- The heroic frame: working-class heroes and victims.

Framing the middle class Three key frames are evident.

- The middle-class values frame: middle class values are the core values of American society to which people should aspire.

- The squeeze frame: the middle class is finding it difficult to maintain its (costly) life style.

- The victimisation frame: middle-class problems are caused by the actions of people from other classes.

All tend to represent the middle class in a positive way, enabling most readers/viewers to identify with this class.

Conclusion Media representations of social classes typically mean that the upper and middle classes are depicted in a positive way and the working class and poor are depicted in a negative way. The result is that the media put forward an ideology which justifies class inequality and 'the ever-widening chasm between the haves and have-nots' (Kendall, 2005).

4.5 Representations of age

Nature and nurture

Over the course of the life cycle, children become teenagers; youths become adults; and middle-aged adults become old. This is normally thought of as a natural process since ageing entails inevitable biological changes. And these biological changes are often accompanied by changes in our attitudes and behaviour. Sociologists, however, argue that these social changes are not just a result of the biological clock ticking away. Indeed the stages themselves – childhood, youth, maturity, old age – have not always been distinguished in the ways we do now (Richardson, 2005).

Childhood Some historians argue that for most of human history children (at least after the age of 6 or 7) were seen as miniature adults. The idea of childhood as a period of innocence and dependence only began to emerge around the 15th century. And even then, the expectation that children should be engaged in education rather than employment took a long while to become the norm. Childhood is now seen as an extended stage of the life cycle and sharply distinguished from adulthood.

Youth For many historians, youth only became recognised as a separate stage of the life cycle after the discovery of childhood. Indeed, it was only in the post-war period that teenagers were affluent enough to become significant consumers of mass media products such as rock and roll, and develop youth cultures. Youth is now recognised to be a stage somewhere between childhood and adulthood.

Adulthood and old age For much of human history, adults were obliged to work for a living until they died. Old age, however, is now seen as a distinct stage in the life cycle when people are entitled to a pension and not expected to be employed.

Representations of age groups

The status of different age groups in Western societies is linked to their economic circumstances. Those in the middle – adults in work – have the most status. By contrast, those at either extremes – the young and the old – whom it is assumed (often incorrectly) do not work, have less status. The different status of age groups results in corresponding variations in mainstream representations. According to McQueen (1998), 'These, broadly, are that: children are helpless and innocent; teenagers irresponsible and rebellious; middle-aged people responsible and conformist; and old people vulnerable and a "burden" on society'. We shall now look at the portrayal of the groups with less status.

*activity*18 *hooligans and yobs*

Item A Hooligans

At twelve—his literary education

At seventeen—a full-fledged Hooligan

From the *Daily Graphic*, 5.12.1900

Item B Yobs

ONE MORE VICTIM OF OUR YOB CULTURE
A father of four was kicked to death by yobs after being asked for a light.

LOUTS DESTROY ANOTHER FAMILY
Britain's yob culture has claimed the life of yet another family man.

ATTACKED BY A TEEN GANG
A barrister was in a coma last night after becoming the latest victim of a teenage street gang. Yobs are intimidating entire neighbourhoods.

Headlines from the *Daily Mail*, June and July 2005

question

What impression of youth is provided by Items A and B?

Children A study of children's television has identified three main strands (McQueen, 1998). The first is a commercial strand and targets children as consumers of cartoons (eg *Tom and Jerry*) and action programmes. The second is a public service strand and seeks to be distinctly educational (eg *Blue Peter*). The third, and most recent, is an adult strand which recognises that children often prefer 'adult' programmes (eg *Neighbours*). In Britain, the second strand – though once dominant – has declined and the third strand has grown. While the former represents children as totally dependent and in need of protection and guidance from adults, the latter recognises diversity among children and their capacity to deal with complex issues.

Youth The most common depiction of young people in the news is the representation of youth as trouble. Hence a series of moral panics in the post-war period about 'depraved youth' who have no respect for authority (Muncie, 1999). Teddy boys were the first 'folk devils' to be identified in the post-war period but they were followed in successive decades by, among others, mods and rockers (see Section 3.2), muggers, punks and joy riders. In each of these cases, a group of young people was identified as trouble. The behaviour of this group in turn served to symbolise what was wrong with youth and, by extension, society generally.

Representing youth in this way – youth as trouble – is not new. An analysis of newspapers over a number of centuries reveals that, in every age, it is common to portray youth as a problem and to contrast contemporary youth with the situation of 20 years ago when young people respected authority and society was in a better state (Pearson, 1983).

Old age Older people are much less likely to be represented on television or in the mass media than younger people, 'with 11 per cent of the population who are aged over 65 years, reduced to only 2.3 per cent of the television population' (McQueen, 1998). When older people are represented, White middle-class men are much more commonly found than women, ethnic minorities or the poor. As for the nature of the images, these are according to one recent account 'overwhelmingly negative, comic or grotesque' (McQueen, 1998).

4.6 Representations of sexuality

The term sexual orientation refers to an individual's sexual preferences – for people of the same sex (homosexuality), persons of the opposite sex (heterosexuality) or persons of either sex (bisexuality). In all societies, there are rules governing what are deemed acceptable sexual relations. While these vary from society to society, in many societies heterosexuality is considered the norm and homosexuality/bisexuality as deviant. Indeed, as late as the 1960s, gay male sexual relations were completely illegal in Britain. And it is only since 2003, with the incorporation into law of the Employment Equality (Sexual Orientation) Regulations, that it has been illegal to discriminate against people because of their sexual orientation. And it was not until 2005 that same-sex couples (lesbians and gays) have been given, through civil partnerships, similar rights as married heterosexual couples.

Representations of lesbians and gay men Analysis of media content has repeatedly produced the following findings.

- Sexual minorities 'mostly…are ignored or denied.
- When they do appear they do so in order to play a supportive role for the natural order and are thus narrowly and negatively stereotyped' (Gross, 1995).
- Common stereotypes include those of 'homosexual men' being 'identified by a mincing walk and camp voices' and 'lesbians…as butch dungaree-wearing feminists' (McQueen, 1998).

Changing representations of sexuality With more societal acceptance of diversity, including diverse sexual orientations, lesbians and gay men have become both more visible and less narrowly and negatively stereotyped. This is evident in a number of ways.

- The greater visibility of gays is evident in advertising, the news and fictional television programmes. Advertisers for example are now more likely to engage in gay-positive marketing campaigns. This is partly in order to attract a previously untapped market – gay consumers – and partly to draw on the perceived hipness of the gay lifestyle in order to sell products to a mass market (Media Awareness Network, 2005).
- In the period from 1981, when AIDS was first identified, to 1985 when a potential AIDS epidemic was recognised, some sections of the press identified gay men as folk devils responsible for what was presented as 'a gay plague'. Gay activists and medical authorities, however, successfully challenged this interpretation of AIDS and indeed persuaded governments after 1986 to develop campaigns in order to promote safe sex (Critcher, 2003).
- While gay men are often represented as camp in situation comedies, less stereotypical representations are evident in soap operas. In contrast to situation comedies and one-off dramas, it is not necessary in soap operas, which comprise an ongoing drama, to identify immediately whether a character is gay. There is room for some character development and it is possible therefore that it may emerge that certain individuals happen to be gay. Despite this, one analysis indicates that plots featuring gays typically 'dealt with the issue of heterosexuals coming to terms with gayness'. In other words, 'media representations are not representing in most cases a gay/lesbian perspective – they are constructed from a heterosexual point of view and aimed at a heterosexual audience' (Bernstein, 2002).
- Although the mainstream media often continue to represent gays and lesbians as the Other, they do present a wider range of images of gay people than was the case. Talk shows provide an opportunity for people outside the sexual mainstream to voice their concerns. And cutting-edge drama series have emerged such as Channel 4's *Queer as Folk* which focused on the lives of three gay men living in Manchester.

activity 19 *double standards*

Item A Censorship?

Tesco has so far been unwilling to sell a new women's magazine, *Scarlet* because its raunchiness is thought to be tasteless and might offend customers. In contrast, equally raunchy lads' weeklies such as *Nuts* and *Zoo* are widely available. Referring to Tesco's decision and to the refusal of many outlets to stock gay and lesbian magazines, the chairperson of Object, an organisation against sexual stereotyping says 'This is social control of women's and gay men's sexual rights by the distributors. Why are male bodies being censored and protected but not women's bodies? Is it because they are afraid of female erotica and homosexuality?'

Adapted from *the Guardian*, 28.11.2005

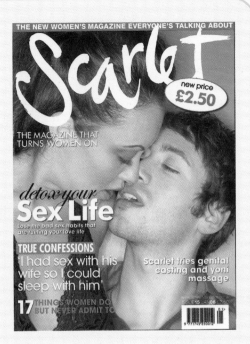

Item B Steering clear

When the American version of *Queer as Folk* was in production, fashion houses such as Versace, Pravda, Polo, Ralph Lauren and Abercrombie & Fitch refused to allow their brands to appear in the series. And although the show is set in Pittsburgh, the marketing director of Pittsburgh Steelers wrote a letter to the producers demanding that all references to the team be removed.

Adapted from *Media Awareness Network*, 2005

questions

1   Look at Item A. What evidence is there of double standards in the treatment of *Scarlet* and *Zoo*?

2   Look at Item B. Why are some companies unwilling to be associated with the drama *Queer as Folk*?

4.7   Representations of disability

There are two main ways of understanding and representing disability:

- The medical model
- The social model.

The medical model This 'views disability as a product of impairment' (Bulsara, 2005). Here the focus is on physical difference such as blindness and being wheelchair bound. The disabled are defined as a group whose bodies do not function normally and who, as a result, are not capable of enjoying an ordinary lifestyle.

The social model By contrast, this model views disability as the outcome of social barriers. Here the focus is on the obstacles and discriminatory practices that people with disabilities face. It is recognised that some people experience impairments, but what is highlighted are the social barriers that prevent these people from enjoying an ordinary lifestyle.

Under-representation of disability

Content analysis of representations of disability on television conducted between 1993 and 2002 indicates that people with disabilities appear infrequently and that there has been little change over the years. In 2002, they made an appearance in 11% of the programmes surveyed but accounted for only 0.8% of all the people who spoke. What is more, the range of disabilities portrayed was very limited, being those highlighted in the medical model, notably blindness and being wheelchair bound (Agyeman, 2003).

Images of the disabled

According to Barnes (1992), there are a range of images of the disabled. Content analysis of both electronic and print media identified the following.

- The disabled person as pitiable and pathetic. Such an image was common on programmes such as *Children in Need* and telethons where the disabled were presented as objects of pity in order for the able-bodied to feel compassion and give money.

- The disabled person as an object of violence, a common scenario in television programmes where disabled people appeared.

- The disabled person as sinister and evil – for example, Shakespeare's *Richard III* or *Treasure Island's* Blind Pew.

- The disabled person as atmosphere or curio – for example, a character with a humped back such as Igor in the film *Frankenstein* being used as a metaphor for evil.

- The disabled person as 'super cripple'. This image of an individual heroically overcoming obstacles is evident in films such as *My Left Foot*, where the central character, Christy Brown is played in fact by an able-bodied actor, a common occurrence in Hollywood films.

- The disabled person as an object of ridicule – for example, Mr Magoo, a partially-sighted cartoon character.

- The disabled person as their own worst enemy able to overcome obstacles if he (or occasionally, she), put their minds to it and ceases to be self pitying.

- The disabled person as a burden who is dependent and needs to be looked after.

- The disabled person as sexually abnormal.

- The disabled person as incapable of participating in community life.

- The disabled person as normal.

While a range of media representations of the disabled can still be identified, the most prevalent ones 'commonly perpetuate negative stereotypes' (Roper, 2003). 'Three potent images are conjured up: pity, dependent and flawed' (Bulsara, 2005). For the most part, media representations thus 'represent disabled people as deviant outsiders in clear juxtaposition to the normal and "able bodied" majority' (Hughes, 1998). While most images of disabled people illustrate that the medical model of disability continues to be dominant, there is little doubt that – as disabled people have become more vocal in their demand for civil rights – more media representations draw upon the social model of disability. In 42% of those cases where people with disabilities appeared on television, for example, issues of prejudice, stereotyping or discrimination were highlighted. It still remains rare, however, for disability to be 'portrayed as an everyday, incidental phenomenon' (Agyeman, 2003) with 'disabled people nipping into the Queen Vic for a drink, and then leaving again' (Furner, 2005).

How important are representations?

The previous sections have demonstrated continuity and change in media representations of different social groups. But how important are these representations? Do they actually influence viewers, listeners and readers?

Their impact cannot be assessed without looking carefully at how audiences respond to the media. The problem here is that people do not respond in a simple and straightforward way to what they see, hear or read. The effects of the mass media on audiences are discussed at length in Unit 5.

summary

1. The mass media represent various social groups. These representations are often based on stereotypes.

2. Studies of gender representations from the 1950s to the 1970s showed that the media presented a stereotype of women as domestic servants and sex objects.

3. More recent evidence indicates that media representations of women are less likely to be based on traditional stereotypes.

4. Media representations of ethnicity have tended to rely on negative stereotypes. Black people were routinely presented as a 'threat' and a 'problem'. Ethnic issues were seen from a White point of view.

5. Recent research indicates more positive representations of minority ethnic groups and a growth in the number and range of representations. However, old stereotypes persist.

6. The working class are under-represented in the media and tend to be pictured in a negative way. The middle class are represented in a more positive light.

7. There has been a move from representing children as dependent and in need of protection to recognising their capacity to deal with complex issues.

8. The most common representation of youth in the news is 'youth as trouble'.

9. Older people are under-represented in the media and tend to be pictured in negative or comic ways.

10. Sexual minorities have tended to be ignored or represented in terms of negative stereotypes. There is some recent evidence of more diverse and positive representations.

11. The disabled are under-represented in the media. Although a range of media images can be identified, the most common continue to reflect negative stereotypes.

12. People do not respond in a straightforward way to what they see, hear and read. As a result, it is difficult to assess the effect of media representations.

Unit 5 Media effects

keyissues

1 What effects do the media have on audiences?

2 Do the media make us more violent?

5.1 Two views of media effects

How do the mass media affect their audiences? There are two main views. The first view sees the media as powerful and their audience as passive. The media are seen to shape the beliefs and behaviour of the audience who passively accept what they see, hear and read and act accordingly. In terms of this view, the audience is pictured as a mass of isolated individuals who are vulnerable to media manipulation and control.

The second view sees an active audience. They use the media to meet their own needs, selecting what they see, hear and read. Rather than simply accepting, they interpret media output, actively constructing their own meanings. And different individuals and groups interpret the media in different ways depending on their individual experiences and group membership.

Research on media effects has tended to swing between these two contrasting views of the audience. However, more recent research has shown a preference for the active audience view.

Hypodermic syringe theory

Early theories of media effects claimed that the mass media have a direct and immediate effect on behaviour. Hypodermic syringe theory likened the effect of the media to the injection of a drug into a vein. The media were seen to have an immediate effect on people's moods and actions. For example, violence in a movie produces feelings of aggression which can lead to violent behaviour.

Evaluation This view pictured a powerful media which could manipulate and control audiences. Much of the evidence used to support hypodermic syringe theory came from laboratory experiments. But the way people behave in laboratories is often very different from their behaviour in real life situations.

activity20 the Martians are coming

Orson Welles broadcasting War of the Worlds

'The girls huddled around their radios trembling and weeping in each other's arms. They separated themselves from their friends only to take their turn at the telephone to make long distance calls to their parents, saying goodbye for what they thought might be the last time. Terror-stricken girls, hoping to escape from the Mars invaders, rushed to the basement of the dormitory.'

With these words, an American college student recalls the reaction of herself and her friends to a radio broadcast in 1938. The broadcast was a radio play by Orson Welles based on H.G. Wells' *War of the Worlds*, a novel about an invasion from Mars. It was so realistic that hundreds of thousands of people, who missed the announcement that it was only a play, were convinced the Martians had invaded. There was widespread panic at the news that millions had been killed by Martian death rays.

Many people just didn't know how to respond. They turned to family and friends to see whether they should believe what they'd heard. They interpreted what they saw in terms of the radio programme. One person looked out of his window and saw that Wyoming Avenue was 'black with cars. People were rushing away, I figured'. Another recounted, 'No cars came down my street. Traffic is jammed on account of the roads being destroyed, I thought.'

Thousands fled towns and cities and took to the hills.

Adapted from Cantril, 1940

New York Times

Radio Listeners in Panic, Taking War Drama as Fact

Many Flee Homes to Escape 'Gas Raid From Mars'—Phone Calls Swamp Police at Broadcast of Wells Fantasy

question

To what extent does the behaviour of the radio audience support the hypodermic syringe theory?

Two-step flow theory

Hypodermic syringe theory largely ignores the fact that people are social beings, that they have families, friends and work colleagues. Katz and Lazarsfeld's influential *two-step flow theory* (1955) emphasised the importance of social relationships in shaping people's response to the media. They argued that opinions are formed in a social context.

Within this context certain people – *opinion leaders* – are influential in shaping the views of others. These individuals are more likely to be exposed to the media, for example to read more newspapers and magazines. As a result, they are more likely to be influenced by the media and, as opinion leaders, to transmit media messages to others. Hence the idea of a two-step flow – attitudes and ideas 'flow *from* radio and print to opinion leaders and *from them* to the less active sections of the population' (Katz and Lazarsfeld, 1955).

Evaluation Two-step flow theory was largely based on research into short-term changes in attitudes and opinions. For example, media presentations of election campaigns were examined in order to discover to what extent they changed people's voting intentions. Often, such studies showed that the media had little effect on people's opinions.

Uses and gratifications theory

The uses and gratifications approach directly challenged the hypodermic syringe theory. Rather than asking what the media do to audiences, it asked what do audiences do with the media. It argued that people use the media to gratify certain needs. To find out what those needs are, you ask people what they get from watching particular programmes. Using this method, McQuail et al. (1972) identified four needs that are met by watching television. The first was escapism, the need for people to forget about everyday problems. The second was companionship, the need to feel in contact with others, for example with characters in a TV soap. The third was personal identity, for example the need to confirm how clever you are by taking part in TV quizzes from your armchair. The fourth was information, the need to know what is going on in the world.

The uses and gratifications approach puts the audience in the driving seat – they choose from what the media has to offer in order to gratify their needs.

Evaluation There are two main criticisms of this view. First, how do we identify audience needs? When people say that television provides escapism, are they saying that is what they want from television or that's what they get from television? Second, are audiences as active in their choice of programmes as the uses and gratifications approach suggests? Here research 'indicates that, for the most part, they are not selective in their choice of viewing' – more often than not, they watch what they're given (McCullagh, 2002).

Cultural effects theory

This theory assumes that the media does have important effects on its audience. These effects are not as immediate and dramatic as those indicated by the hypodermic syringe theory. Nor are they relatively insignificant as suggested by the two-step flow theory. Rather, they can be seen as a slow, steady, long term build-up of ideas and attitudes.

Cultural effects theory assumes that if similar images, ideas and interpretations are broadcast over periods of time, then they may well affect the way we see and understand the world. Thus if television and radio broadcasts, newspapers and magazines all present, for example, a certain image of women, then slowly but surely this will filter into the public consciousness.

Like the two-step flow theory, cultural effects theory recognises the importance of social relationships. It argues that media effects will depend on the social position of members of the audience, for example, their age, gender, class and ethnicity (Glover, 1985).

Evaluation Cultural effects theory is difficult to evaluate. Because the effects it claims take place over long periods of time, it is difficult to show they are a result of media output. They may be due to other factors in the wider society.

Media as texts

This approach states that the media output – TV programmes, films, books, advertisements – can be seen as 'texts' which are 'read' by the audience. The way that these texts are 'written' determines how audiences understand

activity21 *madonna*

question

How would you interpret this image of Madonna?

them. For example, Mulvey (1975) argues that many Hollywood movies encourage us to adopt a 'male gaze' – to identify with male characters and see women as sex objects. This suggests a powerful media which directs audiences to interpret media output in a particular way.

Evaluation This approach pictures a passive audience who simply read 'texts' as they have been 'written'. However, research on audiences suggests that media texts can be read in a variety of ways. As the case studies in the following section indicate, people interpret media output in terms of their personal experience and membership of social groups. For example, their age, gender, ethnicity, sexual orientation, social class and nationality will all influence their interpretation and understanding of the media. John Fiske (1987) uses the example of Madonna's videos to make this point. Researchers might see these videos as reflecting the 'male gaze' with Madonna flaunting her sexuality for the benefit of men and 'teaching young women to see themselves as men would see them'. However, judging

from letters in a teenage magazine, many young girls saw Madonna as a strong, liberated woman who challenged the mainstream model of femininity.

5.2 Case studies of media effects

So far this unit has looked at general theories of media effects. This section looks at case studies which examine how particular audiences respond to particular aspects of media output.

The 1984/5 miners' strike

The 1984/5 miners' strike was regularly reported by the news media. Activity 22 is based on a study by the Glasgow Media Group of television news coverage of the strike (Philo, 1993). The study examines how people interpreted TV news' version of events. It shows that media effects are not simple and direct. Instead, media output is interpreted in various ways in terms of people's beliefs and experiences.

activity22 audience interpretation

Item A *The strike*

Item B *The research*

One hundred and sixty-nine people were interviewed a year after the miners strike of 1984/5. Television news programmes had focused on violent incidents during the strike – clashes between picketing miners and police. Those selected for interview included miners and police who had been involved in the strike, plus a range of people from different parts of the country and with different social backgrounds.

The researchers found that people interpreted the media's version of the strike in terms of their experiences and previously held attitudes and beliefs. 54% of those interviewed believed that the picketing was mostly violent. This reflected media coverage of the strike. However, none of those who had direct knowledge of the strike – the miners and police – believed that picketing was mostly violent. They rejected the impression given by the media. According to them, strikers and police spent most of their time standing round doing nothing.

Adapted from Philo, 1993

questions

1   a) Which picture is typical of the strike?

b) Why do you think TV news focused on violent confrontations?

2   Why did people interpret the news in different ways?

Neighbours – a Punjabi perspective

The Australian soap *Neighbours* was popular with many young people in the Punjabi community in Southall. Research by Marie Gillespie (1995) shows why. *Neighbours* offered the Southall teenagers a picture of family and community life with which to compare their own. Many of them experienced a tension between British and Indian norms and values as they grew up. 'Soap talk' based on *Neighbours* allowed them to contrast, evaluate and criticise their own family life. Many identified with characters in *Neighbours* and appreciated the freedom that young people appeared to have. By comparison, some felt the restrictions of their family were unfair. One girl talks about the emphasis on respect and obedience to elders: 'It drowns your own sense of identity, you can't do what you want, you always have to think of your family honour'. Another girls comments: 'You can see that families in *Neighbours* are more flexible, they do things together as a family, they don't expect that girls should stay at home and do housework and cooking, boys and girls are allowed to mix more freely'.

The young Punjabis interpreted *Neighbours* in terms of their own experiences, concerns and values. This is an important study because it suggests that there are many different audiences 'out there' and that each will interpret media output in a somewhat different way.

Tyneside rappers

Hip-hop/rap is a global music. Yet young people around the world interpret it in terms of their particular meanings and experiences. This can be seen from Andy Bennett's (2001) study of White rappers in Newcastle upon Tyne. They saw hip-hop as a street thing rather than a Black thing. They dropped the 'Americanisms', rapping with local accents, giving accounts of their own lives and dealing with local problems – for example, crack was replaced by Newcastle Brown ale, problems of excessive drinking and alcohol related violence. In their eyes, they created 'pure Geordie rap'.

Again, we see media output being interpreted in terms of the experiences and concerns of a particular audience.

Media effects – conclusion

This unit began with two views of media effects. The first saw the media as powerful and their audience as passive. The media largely shape the beliefs and values of the audience who tend to accept what they see, hear and read. The second view sees the audience as active – selecting and interpreting media output and constructing their own meanings based on individual experience and group membership.

There is evidence to support both views of audience response to media output. For example, the Glasgow Media Group's study of TV news' coverage of the 1984/5 miners' strike found that over half the people interviewed accepted the TV version of events as 'mostly violent'. Summarising the findings of this and other studies, some members of the Glasgow Media Group concluded that in terms of news: 'Most of us, most of the time go along with what the media tell us to be the case' (Eldridge et al., 1997). On the other hand, those who had direct knowledge of the strike rejected the version given by the media.

The case studies examined in this section indicate that audiences are not passive, that their interpretations and meanings are not simply shaped by the media. They bring with them a lifetime of experiences, concerns, expectations and values in terms of which they interpret and give meaning to media output.

summary

1. There are two main views of media effects. The first sees the media as powerful and the audience as passive. The media are seen to shape the beliefs and behaviour of the audience. The second view sees the audience as active – they interpret media output and construct their own meanings.

2. The hypodermic syringe theory sees the media having an immediate and direct effect on people's moods and actions.

3. Two-step flow theory argues that attitudes and ideas flow from the media to opinion leaders to the rest of the population.

4. Uses and gratifications theory argues that people use the media to gratify certain needs – the needs for escapism, companionship, identity and information.

5. Cultural effects theory sees media effects as a slow, steady, long term build-up of beliefs and attitudes in response to the frequent transmission of similar images and ideas over fairly long periods of time.

6. The media as texts approach sees media output as 'texts' which are 'read' by the audience. It argues that the way these texts are 'written' determines how the audience understands them.

7. Case study research shows how particular audiences draw on their beliefs, values, knowledge and experience in order to interpret media output.

activity23 interpreting hip-hop

Item A Dizzy Rascal

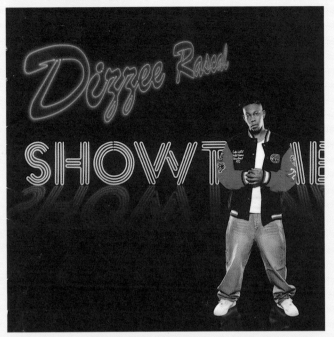

Jay-Z on London Black rapper Dizzy Rascal – 'I like his beats but can't understand a word he says'.

Item B 50 Cent

American rapper 50 Cent performing in Venice, Italy

Item C Chinese hip-hop fans

Chinese hip-hop fans in Beijing

Item D Skinnyman – White London rapper

question

Use these pictures to support the view that hip-hop/rap is interpreted differently by different performers and audiences.

Unit 6 Globalisation

keyissues

1 What is globalisation?
2 What part does the media play in the process of globalisation?

6.1 What is globalisation?

Many sociologists believe that a process known as *globalisation* is occurring. Communication is often on a global scale. As a result, we are increasingly aware of events occurring across the globe. The world appears to be shrinking.

A key feature of globalisation is *time-space compression* – time seems to be quickening up and space seems to be getting smaller. This is partly due to the development of information and communications technology. For example, the computerisation of financial markets enables vast amounts of money to be transferred rapidly from one side of the world to the other. And communication satellites allow instant communication across the globe. As a result, events occurring thousands of miles away can have an immediate impact as time and space are increasingly compressed.

Global village The Live Aid movement of the mid-1980s provides a good example of the way that the world has come to seem more like a village. The movement, founded by the singer Bob Geldof, emerged in order to raise money to relieve an appalling famine in Ethiopia. Its highlight was a day-long concert, held at venues in Britain and America 3,000 miles apart, and linked by satellite into one programme. The mass media were central. It was television which allowed people in Britain and America to become aware of a famine thousands of miles away. And it was television which broadcast the concert around the world.

Spaceship earth The explosion in 1986 at the Chernobyl nuclear plant in the former Soviet Republic of Ukraine provides a dramatic example of our ecological interdependence on spaceship earth. The consequences of the explosion were felt as far away as Cumbria. The explosion provides an example of the way in which the very survival of the planet is threatened by the use of certain technological developments. Media coverage across the world made many people realise that they shared their fate with everyone else on the planet.

The medium as the message The media played a key role in both Live Aid and Chernobyl. Live Aid would not have happened without the media and we might not have heard about Chernobyl without media coverage. Media technologies are crucial in creating a shrinking world.

activity24 *a shrinking world*

Item A 9-11

Attack on the World Trade Center, New York, September 11, 2001

Item B David Beckham

David Beckham escorted through a cheering crowd in China. It is estimated that a billion Chinese watched his debut for Real Madrid against the all-star Chinese Dragons in Beijing on August 3, 2003.

question

How do these items suggest that we are living in a shrinking world?

Some writers go further and argue that the content of media messages has always been less important than the media technologies used for conveying messages (McLuhan, 1994). Take, for example, the invention in the fifteenth century of a printing process using movable metal type. This enabled books to be produced more cheaply. Publishers initially produced books in Latin but the market for such works was limited. Keen to expand their market, publishers produced translations in local languages. The increased availability of books, along with the establishment of newspapers in the eighteenth century, helped to standardise and spread these languages. 'For the first time, it was possible for the mass of people within a particular state to understand each other through a common print language' (Barker, 1999). In this way, the print media enabled people to develop a common national identity.

For McLuhan and his followers, the significance of the new media, like satellite broadcasting and the Internet, is that they bring people closer together and enable people to see themselves as members of a 'global village'. While an earlier print technology encouraged identification with the nation, the new technologies encourage identification with the global village.

Evaluation McLuhan's emphasis on media technology – the medium is the message – has been criticised. New technologies don't operate in a vacuum. What sociologists stress is the need to examine the social context within which they operate. Which technologies are developed and how they are used depends upon economic and political factors. The private and increasingly concentrated ownership of media industries, coupled with increasing reliance on the market, are now the key economic and political factors shaping the development of the media.

New technologies create a range of opportunities. The new media *may* encourage people to see themselves as members of a global village, but whether this happens will depend upon other factors. The Internet provides opportunities across the globe for both commercial gain and public debate. The context within which the Internet has recently developed means, however, that the 'trend towards the commercialisation of the web is becoming the dominant one' (McCullagh, 2002).

6.2 Globalisation and the media

The global context of the media has the following characteristics.

- Across the world, a small number of transnational media organisations have emerged. Organisations such as AOL Time Warner, Disney, Viacom and News Corporation operate at a global level in terms of the production, distribution and sale of their media products.

- Unlike traditional publicly or privately owned media organisations, transnational media organisations operate in an increasingly deregulated environment. They face few regulations preventing them from focusing their activities on purely commercial considerations.

- The major transnational organisations, whose main base is in Western societies, dominate the global network of communication. It is the images, music and words of Western societies that are most commonly found in media around the world (Devereux, 2003).

Media imperialism Some sociologists argue that the power of transnational media organisations across the world is so great that we are witnessing a new form of *imperialism* – a new type of empire. While the direct political control of one nation by another is no longer very common, media organisations are transmitting Western values and attitudes across the world. 'The global television music of MTV, the global news of CNN, the global box office hits of Hollywood films and the global television soap operas shape the cultures of the global South, ensuring their Westernisation' (Williams, 2003). The media imperialism view claims that the flow of Western media products across the world means that local cultures will be battered into submission and disintegrate.

Evaluation Many sociologists reject the view of media imperialism. For example, Giddens (1990) argues that globalisation does not necessarily lead to a Westernised world which watches Hollywood movies, listens to rap music, and takes its lead from Western role models in films and on TV.

Even when the same television programmes are shown around the world, people don't necessarily respond to them in the same way. For example, Dutch viewers enjoyed the glossy US soap opera *Dallas*, but rejected the programme's celebration of the values of American capitalism (Ang, 1985). And even if the rights to programmes such as *Who wants to be a millionaire?* and *Big Brother* are sold to TV companies across the world, local versions reflecting local cultures are produced.

Resisting media imperialism Sreberny-Mohammadi (1996) points to a number of ways in which local cultures resist media imperialism.

- Home-produced programmes can replace imports because they are more attractive to local audiences for cultural reasons. Research in Asia, for example, showed that in seven of nine countries more hours of locally produced television were broadcast than of imported programmes (Gorman & McLean, 2003).

- In some cases, the flow of programmes may be reversed so that local programmes are exported to Western societies. For example, British Asians 'maintain strong ties with their countries of origin through the consumption of popular film and television exported from the Indian sub-continent' (Gillespie, 1995).

- Local producers can create transnational media organisations. For example, ZEE TV, a Hindi-language commercial station, took over TV Asia in Britain.

- In many countries, there are attempts to restrict foreign imports, to block access to foreign websites and even ban the sale of satellite dishes.

activity25 media imperialism

Buying pirated videos and DVDs in Shanghai, China. Titles include Gone With The Wind and Disney's Sleeping Beauty.

Vietnamese edition of 8 Mile and Russian edition of Lord of the Rings

MTV Asia Singles Chart

question

How do these items support the claim that the media are spreading Western tastes and values across the world?

We should not romanticise these forms of resistance. In some cases, restricting foreign imports and banning the sale of satellite dishes has less to do with seeking to preserve local cultures and more to do with maintaining power. For example, foreign programmes promoting a more liberated image of women may be seen as a threat by men in some societies. At the same time, we need to recognise the global context within which resistance occurs. There may be a two-way flow of media products, but that flow is not an equal one. Richer countries not only have greater access to the new media. They are also the places where the major media organisations are owned and directed.

key terms

Globalisation The process by which the various countries and cultures across the world become more closely intertwined.

Time-space compression The process by which time seems to be quickening up and space seems to be getting smaller.

Global village The idea that the world seems increasingly like a village.

Spaceship earth A view which looks down on the world and sees it like a spaceship populated by all the people on earth.

Media imperialism The idea that Western-owned transnational media organisations are like a new type of empire with power over the large sections of the world.

summary

1. The media are an important part of the process of globalisation.

2. According to McLuhan, new media technologies encourage people to identify with the 'global village'.

3. Other researchers admit that new media technologies are important, but place more emphasis on the economic and political context in which they operate. For example, the new technologies are used by transnational media organisations for commercial purposes.

4. The dominant position of Western media organisations has led some researchers to see this as media imperialism.

5. However, the flow of ideas and opinions is not simply one way. There are plenty of locally-produced media products, some of which are exported to Western countries.

Unit 7 *Postmodernism*

keyissues

1 How do postmodernists see today's society?

2 What is the role of the media in postmodern society?

7.1 Postmodern society and the media

Some researchers believe we are living in a *postmodern society*, a society that comes after and is different from modern society. This new age is known as *postmodernity*. Those who take this view are known as *postmodernists*. This section looks at some of the key features of postmodern society and their relationship to the media.

Media realities

Multiple realities We live in a media-saturated society. The media bombard us with images which increasingly dominate the way we see ourselves and the world around us. Media images, it is argued, do not reflect or even distort social reality. They are themselves realities. Our consciousness is invaded by the *multiple realities* provided by news, documentaries, pop music, advertisements, soaps and movies set in the past, present and future, on this world and other worlds.

The media not only provide multiple views of reality – these views are also open to a multitude of different interpretations. Media audiences are active – individuals place their own interpretations on what they see, hear and read.

Simulation Increasing exposure to the media blurs the division between our everyday reality and media images. The media provide us with much of our knowledge about the world. But this knowledge is not drawn from our direct experience. Instead it is reproduced knowledge, it is a *simulation* – it represents the real thing but it is not a true or genuine representation. In this sense, it has similarities to a *Playstation* game.

To some extent, postmodernists apply this view to every aspect of the media – from the news, to soaps, to advertisements. From this perspective media simulations remove the distinction between image and reality – images become part of our reality.

Multiple truths As a result of the multiple realities and the variety of simulations presented by the media, the idea of an absolute truth has gone. There is no longer a single dominant meaning. Instead there are a multitude of meanings. A single truth has been replaced by many truths as the media broadcast different perspectives and different views from across the world and from the past and the present.

Living the image Images we experience from the media become as, if not more, real and significant than things we directly experience in everyday life. For example, the death of Princess Diana resulted in an outpouring of grief across the world – but for the vast majority she existed only through the media. And the same applies to the footballer George Best. His image was kept alive by the media and his death was headlined by TV news and national newspapers.

Even fiction can become 'real'. A death, a divorce or a marriage in a soap opera glues millions to the screen and is talked about next day as if it actually happened. As its name suggests, reality TV brings 'real' people into our homes and conversations. And it sometimes draws audiences further into this reality as they vote for which participants are to stay or go in shows like *Big Brother* and *I'm A Celebrity, Get Me Out Of Here*.

Postmodern identies

Identity and choice In modern societies, people's identities were usually drawn from their class, gender, occupation and ethnic group. In postmodern society, people have more opportunity to construct their own identities and more options to choose from. For example, a woman can be heterosexual, bisexual or lesbian, a business executive and a mother, she can be British, a Sikh and a member of Greenpeace. And her lifestyle and consumption patterns can reflect her chosen identity. Brand-name goods such as Gucci and Dolce & Gabbana can be used as statements of her identity.

With all the choices on offer, it is fairly easy for people to change their identities, or to have several identities which they put on and take off depending on their social situation. As a result, postmodern identities are more unstable and fragile. They offer choice, but they don't always provide a firm and lasting foundation.

Identity and the media The media offer a wide range of identities and lifestyles from which we can pick and choose and act out. Adverts sell images and style rather than content and substance. Jeans are not marketed as hard wearing and value for money but rather as style in the context of rock, R&B or hip-hop music. Drinks like Tango, Bacardi and Smirnoff Ice are sold on style and image rather than taste or quality. Coca-Cola is the 'real thing' despite the fact that it mainly consists of coloured sweetened water.

According to postmodernists, people are increasingly constructing their own identities from images and lifestyles presented by the media.

Time, space and change

Time and space The media allow us to criss-cross time and space. *Romeo and Juliet* was written by Shakespeare in the 16th century but the film starring Leonardo di Caprio takes place in the present day. Watching TV news we can go round the world in 30 minutes from Iraq to the USA, from Afghanistan to Northern Ireland. Adverts use music from the 1950s, 60s and 70s to sell beer, washing powder and jeans. And fashions in clothes, such as Miss Sixty, recreate styles from the past. As a result, 'time and space become less stable and comprehensible, more confused, more incoherent, more disunified' (Strinati, 1992)

Change Images and styles are constantly changing. The media regularly present new styles of music and fashion, new types of food and drink, new and improved household products, many of which are linked to new lifestyles. Often these products are associated with media personalities – for example, Glow by JLO, advertised as 'the new fragrance by Jennifer Lopez'.

As a result of this constant change and emphasis on the new, things appear fluid – nothing seems permanent and solid. The mainstream culture of modern society is replaced by the fleeting, unstable, fragmented culture of postmodern society.

7.2 Postmodernism and the media – evaluation

Many sociologists are critical of the picture of the media and society presented by postmodernists. Greg Philo and David Miller (2001) make the following points.

- There is no way of saying that reality is distorted by media images because, according to postmodernists, those images and the way that people interpret them are the reality. This is carrying the idea of an active audience to a ridiculous extreme.

- People are well aware that there is a reality beyond the images broadcast by the media. They recognise that media messages are often one-sided, partial and distorted.

- Many people are not free to construct their own identities and select their own lifestyles. For example, people living in poverty simply don't have the money to buy Gucci sunglasses or Jean Paul Gaultier fragrance.

Despite these criticisms, many sociologists accept that the media are increasingly influential in today's society. And they accept that there is something to many of the points made by postmodernists, but see their argument as going too far.

*activity*26 *postmodernism and the media*

Item A *Identity cards*

Will it ever come to this? The Government is planning to sell Identity Scratch Cards. Scratch off the special square and you may win a year's worth of free identity. The winner gets to choose a dream identity, for example, a pop star or a major sports personality.

Adapted from Iannucci, 1995

Item B *Image and style*

Item C *The Truman Show*

In the film *The Truman Show* a man discovers that his life has been constructed as a soap opera. His family, friends and neighbours are all actors and he is the central character. Everything around him is an illusion, created by the media.

question

How do these items illustrate the postmodernist view of the media and society?

key terms

Postmodern society A society that comes after and is different from modern society.

Postmodernists Researchers who argue that we now live in a postmodern age.

Multiple realities The idea that the media present a number of different realities.

Simulation Images projected by the media rather than drawn from our direct experience. Despite this, these images become part of our reality.

summary

1. According to postmodernists, we live in a media-saturated society.
2. The media bombard us with multiple realities. These realities are simulations. Despite this, they become part of our reality. As a result, the division between everyday reality and media images disappears.
3. A single truth becomes multiple truths as the media present different views from across the world.
4. The media offer a wide range of identities and lifestyles from which we can pick and choose.
5. The media constantly present new images and styles. As a result, nothing seems permanent and solid.
6. Many critics argue that postmodernists have overstated their case, but accept there is something in what they say.

References

Abercrombie, N. (1996). *Television and society.* Cambridge: Polity.

Agyeman, L. (2003). *End of year report: BSC and ITC research 2003.* London: Broadcasting Standards Commission & Independent Television Commission.

Allan, S. (1999). *News culture.* Buckingham: Open University Press.

Allport, G.W. & Postman, L. (1947). *The psychology of rumour.* New York: H. Holt & Company.

Ang, I. (1985). *Watching 'Dallas': Soap opera and the melodramatic imagination.* London: Methuen.

Bagdikian, B. (2004). *The new media monopoly.* Boston: Beacon Press.

Barker, C. (1999). *Television, globalisation and cultural identities.* Buckingham: Open University Press.

Barnes, C. (1992). *Disabling imagery and the media.* London: Ryburn Press.

Bennett, A. (2001). Local interpretations of global music. In N. Abercrombie & A. Warde (Eds.), *The contemporary British society reader.* Cambridge: Polity Press.

Bernstein, A. (2002). Representation, identity and the media. In C. Newbold, O.Boyd-Barrett & H. van Den Bulck (Eds.), *The media book.* London: Arnold.

Buckingham, D. (1996). *Moving images: Understanding children's emotional responses to television.* Manchester: Manchester University Press.

Bulsara, A. (2005). *Depictions of people with disabilities in the British media,* www.media-diversity.org.

Burton, G. (2005). *Media and society: Critical perspectives.* Maidenhead: Open University Press.

Butsch, R. (1995). Ralph, Fred, Archie and Homer: Why television keeps recreating the white male working-class buffoons. In G. Dines & J. Humez (Eds.), *Gender, race and class in media.* London: Sage.

Cantril, H. (1940). *The invasion from Mars: A study in the psychology of panic.* New York: Harper & Row.

Castells, M. (1996). *The rise of network society.* Oxford: Blackwell.

Cohen, S. (1987). *Folk devils and moral panics.* Oxford: Blackwell.

Collins, R. & Murroni, C. (1996). *New media, new politics.* Oxford: Polity Press.

Cottle, S. (Ed.) (2000). *Ethnic minorities and the media.* Buckingham: Open University Press.

Cowe, R. (2001). The acceptable face of anti-capitalism. *The Observer,* 6 May.

Critcher, C. (2003). *Moral panics and the media.* Buckingham: Open University Press.

Croteau, D. & Hoynes, W. (1997). *Media/society.* London: Forge Pine Press.

Curran, J. & Seaton, J. (1997). *Power without responsibility.* London: Routledge.

Daniels, T. (1996). Programmes for Black audiences. In J. Corner & S. Harvey (Eds.), *Television times.* London: Arnold.

Devereux, E. (2003). *Understanding the media.* London: Sage.

Dobson, A. (1992). Ideology. *Politics Review,* vol 1.4.

Dodd, K. & Dodd, P. (1992). From the East End to *EastEnders.* In D. Strinati & S. Wagg (Eds.), *Come on down: Popular media culture.* London: Routledge.

Ehrenreich, B. (1995). The silenced majority: Why the average working person has disappeared from American media and culture. In G. Dines & J. Humez (Eds.), *Gender, race and class in media.* London: Sage.

Eldridge, J. (1995). *Getting the message: News, truth and power.* London: Routledge.

Eldridge, J., Kitzinger, J. & Williams, K. (1997). *The mass media and power in modern Britain.* Oxford: Oxford University Press.

Ferguson, M. (1983). *Forever feminine.* London: Heinemann.

Fiske, J. (1987). *Television culture.* London: Methuen.

Franklin, B. (1997). *Newszak and news media.* London: Arnold.

Furner, B. (2005). How are we looking? *The Guardian.*

Gauntlett, D. (2002). *Media, gender and identity.* London: Routledge.

Giddens, A. (1990). *The consequences of modernity.* Cambridge: Polity Press.

Gilbert, G.M. (1951). Stereotype persistence and change among college students. *Journal of Abnormal and Social Psychology, 46,* 245-254.

Gillespie, M. (1995). *Television, ethnicity and cultural change.* London: Routledge.

Gillespie, M. (2002). *From comic Asians to Asian comics.* London: BFI.

Glasgow Media Group (1997). *Ethnic minorities in television advertising.* Glasgow: GMG.

Glover, D. (1985). The sociology of the mass media. In M. Haralambos (Ed.), *Sociology: New Directions.* Ormskirk: Causeway Press.

Golding, P. & Middleton, S. (1982). *Images of welfare: Press and public attitudes to poverty.* Oxford: Blackwell.

Goode, E. & Ben-Yehuda, N. (1994). *Moral panics: The social construction of deviance.* Oxford: Blackwell.

Gorman, L. & McLean, D. (2003). *Media and society in the twentieth century.* Oxford: Blackwell.

Graber, D.A., Bimber, B. Bennett, W.L., Davis, R. & Norris, P. (2004). The Internet and politics: Emerging perspectives. In N. Nissenbaum & M.E. Price (Eds.), *Academy and the Internet.* New York: Peter Lang.

Gross, L. (1995). Out of the mainstream: Sexual minorities and the mass media. In G. Dines & J. Humez (Eds.), *Gender, race and class in media.* London: Sage.

Habermas, J. (1992). Further reflections on the public sphere. In C. Calhoun (Ed.), *Habermas and the public sphere.* Cambridge, MA: MIT Press.

Hall, S. (1995). The whites of their eyes. In G. Dines & J. Humez (Eds.), *Gender, race and class in media.* London: Sage.

Hall, S. (1997). The spectacle of the 'other'. In S. Hall (Ed.), *Representation: Cultural representations and signifying practices.* London: Sage.

Hall, S., Critcher, C., Jefferson, T., Clarke, J. & Roberts, B. (1978). *Policing the crisis.* London: Macmillan.

Harris, M. (1984). The strange saga of the Video Bill. *New Society,* 26 April, 140-142.

Herman, E. & Chomsky, N. (1988). *The political economy of the mass media.* New York: Pantheon Books.

Hetherington, A. (1985). *News, newspapers and television.* London: Macmillan.

Heywood, A. (2002). *Politics* (2nd ed.). Basingstoke: Palgrave.

Higson, A. (1998). National identity and the media. In A. Briggs & P. Cobley (Eds.), *The media: An introduction.* Harlow: Longman.

Hughes, G. (1998). Constructions of disability. In E. Saraga (Ed.), *Embodying the social: Constructions of difference.* London: Routledge.

Iannucci, A. (1995). Play your card right. *The Guardian,* May 2.

Karlins, M., Coffman, T.L. & Walters, G. (1969). On the fading of social stereotypes: Studies in three generations of college students. *Journal of Personality and Social Psychology, 13,* 1-16.

Katz, D. & Braly, K.W. (1933). Racial stereotypes of 100 college students. *Journal of Abnormal and Social Psychology, 28,* 280-290.

Katz, E. & Lazarsfeld, P. (1955). *Personal influence.* New York: Free Press.

Kendall, D. (2005). *Framing class.* Lenham: Rowman & Littlefield.

Law, I. (1997). *Privilege and silence: 'Race' in the British news during the general election campaign, 1997.* Leeds: University of Leeds.

Livingstone, S. (2004). The challenge of changing audiences: Or, what is the audience researcher to do in the Internet age? *European Journal of Communication, 19,* 75-86.

Marcuse, H. (1964). *One dimensional man.* London: Routledge & Kegan Paul.

McCullagh, C. (2002). *Media power.* Basingstoke: Palgrave.

McLuhan, M. (1994). *Understanding media: The extensions of man.* London: Routledge.

McNair, B. (1996). *News and journalism in the UK.* London: Routledge.

McQuail, D., Blumler, J. & Brown, R. (1972). The television audience: A revised perspective. In D. McQuail (Ed.), *Sociology of mass communication*. Harmondsworth: Penguin.

McQueen, D. (1998). *Television: A media student's guide*. London: Arnold.

McRobbie, A. (1999). *In the culture society: Art, fashion and popular music*. London: Routledge.

Media Awareness Network (2005). *Representations of gays and lesbians on television*. www.media-awareness.ca

Miliband, R. (1973). *The state in capitalist society*. London: Quartet Books.

Mulvey, L. (1975). Visual pleasure and narrative cinema. *Screen, 16*, (3).

Muncie, J. (1999). *Youth and crime*. London: Sage.

Murdock, G. (1992). Embedded persuasions: The fall and rise of integrated advertising. In D. Strinati & S. Wagg (Eds.), *Come on down: Popular media culture*. London: Routledge.

Negrine, R. (1994). *Politics and the mass media in Britain*. London: Routledge.

Neill, A. (1996). *Full disclosure*. London: Macmillan.

Newbold, C., Boyd-Barrett, O. & Van Den Bulk, H. (Eds.), (2002). *The Media Book*. London: Arnold.

Norris, P. (2001). *Digital divide: Civic engagement, information poverty and the Internet worldwide*. Cambridge: Cambridge University Press.

Peake, S. (2002). *The Guardian media guide 2003*. London: Atlantic Books.

Pearson, G. (1983). *Hooligan: A history of respectable fears*. London: Macmillan.

Philo, G. & Miller, D. (Eds.) (2001). *Market killing: What the free market does and what social scientists can do about it*. Harlow: Longman.

Philo, G. & Miller, D. (2002). Circuits of communication and power: Recent developments in media sociology. In M. Holborn (Ed.), *Developments in Sociology, Volume 18*. Ormskirk: Causeway Press.

Philo, G. (1993). Getting the message: Audience research in the Glasgow University Media Group. In J. Eldridge (Ed.), *Getting the message: News truth and power*. London: Routledge.

Reeves, R. (1999). Inside the world of the global protestors. *The Observer*, 31 October.

Richardson, J. (2005). *Youth and culture for OCR*. Ormskirk: Causeway Press.

Roper, L. (2003). *Disability in media*, www.mediaed.org.uk

Ross, K. (1996). *Black and White media*. Cambridge: Polity Press.

Schlesinger, P. (1991). *Media, state and nation*. London: Sage.

Schudson, M. (2000). The sociology of news production revisited – again. In J. Curran & M. Gurevitch (Eds.), *Mass media and society*. London: Arnold.

Solomos, J. & Back, L. (1996). *Racism and society*. London: Macmillan.

Sreberny-Mohammadi, A. (1996). The global and local in international communication. In J. Curran & M. Gurevitch (Eds.), *Mass media and society*. London: Arnold.

Strinati, D. (1992). Postmodernism and popular culture. *Sociology Review*, April.

Tuchman, G. (1978). *Making news*. New York: Free Press.

Tuchman, G. (1981). The symbolic annihilation of women by the mass media. In S. Cohen & J. Young (Eds.), *The manufacture of news*. London: Constable.

Tunstall, J. (1983). *The media in Britain*. London: Constable.

Van Dijk, T. (1991). *Racism and the press*. London: Routledge.

Williams, K. (2003). *Understanding media theory*. London: Arnold.

Author index

A

Abercrombie, N. 31, 33
Agyeman, L. 39, 40
Allan, S. 22, 25
Allport, G.W. 29
Ang, I. 47

B

Back, L. 33
Bagdikian, B. 7, 10, 14
Barker, C. 47
Barnes, C. 39
Bennett, A. 44
Bennett, W.L. 18
Ben-Yehuda, N. 26, 28
Bernstein, A. 38
Bimber, D. 18
Blumler, J. 42
Boyd-Barrett, O. 6, 32
Braly, K.W. 30
Brown, R. 42
Bulsara, A. 39, 40
Burton, G. 24
Butsch, R. 35

C

Cantril, H. 41
Castells, M. 20

Chomsky, N. 10
Clarke, J. 23
Coffman, T.L. 30
Cohen, S. 25
Collins, R. 17
Cottle, S. 33
Cowe, R. 19
Critcher, C. 23, 26, 27, 28, 38
Croteau, D. 6
Curran, J. 8, 10

D

Daniels, T. 33
Davis, R. 18
Devereux, E. 5, 47
Dobson, A. 16
Dodd, K. 36
Dodd, P. 36

E

Ehrenreich, B. 35
Eldridge, J. 11, 35, 44

F

Ferguson, M. 32
Fiske, J. 43
Franklin, B. 10
Furner, B. 40

G

Gauntlett, D. 31, 32
Giddens, A. 47
Gilbert, G.M. 30
Gillespie, M. 35, 44, 47
Glover, D. 42
Golding, P. 36
Goode, E. 26, 28
Gorman, L. 17, 20, 47
Graber, D.A. 18
Gramsci, A. 13
Gross, L. 38

H

Habermas, J. 17
Hall, S. 14, 23, 33
Hall, S. 33
Harris, M. 27
Herman, E. 10
Hetherington, A. 22
Heywood, A. 16
Higson, A. 33
Hoynes, W. 6
Hughes, G. 40

I

Iannucci, A. 50

J
Jefferson, T. 23

K
Karlins, M. 30
Katz, D. 30
Katz, E. 42
Kendall, D. 36, 37
Kitzinger, J. 11, 44

L
Law, I. 34
Lazarsfeld, P. 42
Lippman, W. 29
Livingstone, S. 18

M
Marcuse, H. 13
McCullagh, C. 4, 10, 22, 24, 42, 47
McLean, D. 17, 20, 47
McLuhan, M. 47, 48
McNair, B. 23
McQuail, D. 42
McQueen, D. 37, 38

McRobbie, A. 32
Middleton, S. 36
Miliband, R. 13
Miller, D. 24, 50
Mulvey, L. 43
Muncie, J. 38
Murdock, G. 10
Murroni, C. 17

N
Negrine, R. 17
Neill, A. 12
Newbold, C. 6, 32
Norris, P. 18

P
Peake, S. 6, 7, 17
Pearson, G. 38
Philo, G. 24, 43, 44, 50
Postman, L. 29

R
Reeves, R. 19
Richardson, J. 37

Roberts, B. 23
Roper, L. 40
Ross, K. 33

S
Schlesinger, P. 24
Schudson, M. 24
Seaton, J. 8, 10
Solomos, J. 33
Sreberny-Mohammadi, A. 47
Strinati, D. 50

T
Tuchman, G. 22, 30
Tunstall, J. 30, 31

V
Van Den Bulk, H. 6, 32
Van Dijk, T. 33

W
Walters, G. 30
Williams, K. 6, 11, 22, 44, 47

Subject index

A
advertising 10
    ethnicity and 33
    gender and 31-32
age groups
    representations of 26, 37
anti-capitalist movement 19
AOL Time Warner 6, 7, 20, 47

B
Bertelsmann 7
blogs 17

C
cable television 17
class, social
    Marxist views on 13-14
    representations of 35-37
concentration (of media organisations) 6, 7, 8, 10, 12
cultural effects theory 42
cultural hegemony 13-14

D
democracy 8, 10, 16, 17-20
deregulation 8-9, 12
digital divide 18, 20
digitalisation 17
disability
    representation of 39-40
Disney 6, 7, 47

E
e-commerce 16, 20-21
e-democracy 16, 18-20
ethnicity 9
    representations of 33-35

F
Fahrenheit 9/11 15
false consciousness 13
feminism 16
folk devils 25

G
gatekeepers 22
gender 9, 16
    representations of 30-32
globalisation 46-48

H
hip-hop 44, 45
horizontal integration 6
Hurricane Katrina 15
hypodermic syringe theory 41

I
identity 49
ideology 13-14, 16
    cultural hegemony and 13-14
    feminist views 16
    liberal views 16
    Marxist views 13-14
    neutral views 16
    patriarchal 16
    political 16
    ruling class 13-14
instrumental approach 10
Internet 17, 18-21
liberal ideology 16

M
Marxism 10-12
mass media
    as a public sphere 17-18

concentration of 6, 7, 8, 10, 12
definitions of 4
democracy and 8, 10, 16, 17-20
deregulation of 8-9, 12
effects 41-45
globalisation and 46-48
horizontal integration of 6
ideology and 13-14, 16
in postmodern society 49-51
Marxism and 10-12
moral panics and 25-27
new 16-21
news production and 22-28
organisations 5
ownership and control of 6, 7, 8-15
pluralism and 8-12
postmodernism and 49-51
proprietors influence on 10-12
representations 29-40
transnational companies and 6
vertical integration of 6
media as texts 42-43
media imperialism 47-48
miners' strike 43-44
moral panics 25-27
multiple realities 49
multiple truths 49

N
new media 16-21
news 22-28
    class, social and 35-36
    ethnicity and 33-34
    frameworks 23, 25
    influence of media workers on 22-24
    influence of organisational
        structures on 22-24

influence of proprietors on 10-12
influence of wider culture on 24
moral panics and 25-27
objectivity 22-23
values 22, 23-24
News Corporation 7, 11-12, 47
news values 22, 23-24

O

ownership and control 6, 7, 8-15

P

patriarchal ideology 16, 31
pluralism 8-12
postmodern identities 49
postmodern society 49-51
postmodernism 49-51
primary definers 23
proprietors 10-12
public sphere 17-18

R

racism 33
rap 44, 45
representations 29-40
        of age groups 26, 37-38
        of class, social 35-37
        of disability 39-40
        of ethnicity 33-35
        of gender 30-32
        of sexuality 38-39
ruling class ideology 13-14, 16

S

satellite broadcasting 17
sexuality
        representations of 38-39
social class (see class, social)
stereotypes 29-30, 31-32, 33
structural approach 10

T

transnational companies 6, 47
two-step flow theory 42

U

uses and gratifications theory 42

V

vertical integration 6
Viacom 7, 47

Z

Zapatistas 19